Winning Wrestling Moves

Mark Mysnyk, MD

Barry Davis
Head Coach, University of Wisconsin

Brooks Simpson
Coach, Parkview High School, Springfield, Missouri

Human Kinetics

Library of Congress Cataloging-in-Publication Data

Mysnyk, Mark.
Winning wrestling moves / Mark Mysnyk, Barry Davis, Brooks Simpson.
p. cm.
Includes index.
ISBN: 0-87322-482-5
1. Wrestling. I. Davis, Barry, 1967- II. Simpson, Brooks.
III. Title.
GV1195.M96 1994
796.8'12--dc20 93-42161
CIP

ISBN-10: 0-87322-482-5
ISBN-13: 978-0-87322-482-6

Acquisitions Editor: Brian Holding; **Developmental Editors:** Ann Brodsky and Larret Galasyn-Wright; **Assistant Editors:** Lisa Sotirelis, Dawn Roselund, and John Wentworth; **Copyeditor:** Tom Rice; **Proofreader:** Karen Leszczynski; **Production Director:** Ernie Noa; **Book Designer:** Doug Burnett; **Cover Designer:** Jack Davis; **Cover Photographer:** Rodney White/Iowa City Press-Citizen; **Interior Photographers:** Wayne Johnson and Steve Yagla; **Printer:** United Graphics

Human Kinetics books are available at special discounts for bulk purchase. Special editions or book excerpts can also be created to specification. For details, contact the Special Sales Manager at Human Kinetics.

Printed in the United States of America 20 19

Human Kinetics
Web site: www.HumanKinetics.com

United States: Human Kinetics
P.O. Box 5076
Champaign, IL 61825-5076
800-747-4457
e-mail: humank@hkusa.com

Canada: Human Kinetics
475 Devonshire Road Unit 100
Windsor, ON N8Y 2L5
800-465-7301 (in Canada only)
e-mail: orders@hkcanada.com

Europe: Human Kinetics
107 Bradford Road
Stanningley
Leeds LS28 6AT, United Kingdom
+44 (0) 113 255 5665
e-mail: hk@hkeurope.com

Australia: Human Kinetics
57A Price Avenue
Lower Mitcham, South Australia 5062
08 8277 1555
e-mail: liaw@hkaustralia.com

New Zealand: Human Kinetics
Division of Sports Distributors NZ Ltd.
P.O. Box 300 226 Albany
North Shore City
Auckland
0064 9 448 1207
e-mail: info@humankinetics.co.nz

Contents

Foreword

When Mark Mysnyk asked me to write the foreword to *Wrestling Fundamentals and Techniques* back in 1982, I would never have imagined that a dozen years later I'd be writing another foreword for Mark. But now he's come out with a book that's even better than his original work. Not only have Mark and his co-authors Barry Davis and Brooks Simpson updated the book with more than 200 new moves, they also have added detail and clarification to the old moves, using all new photographs throughout.

Mark turned to the University of Iowa's wrestling program for input on the book. To make sure that this was a complete and technically correct resource, he enlisted the help of two former Hawkeye stars, Barry Davis and Brooks Simpson. Barry was a three-time National Collegiate Champion and Olympic medalist, and after assistant coaching at Iowa is now the head coach at the University of Wisconsin. Brooks achieved All-America status at Iowa, and is now applying his coaching skills at the high school level.

No matter how good a wrestler or coach you are, you need to be fundamentally sound and to stay current. That's what I've always tried to do to stay one notch ahead of the competition. Whether you're a wrestler or a coach, *Winning Wrestling Moves* can give you the advantage you need to come out on top!

Dan Gable
Olympic and World Champion Wrestler
Former Olympic Coach
University of Iowa Wrestling Coach and
Coach of 12 NCAA Championship Teams

Preface

Wrestling is a sport of moves and countermoves. The more techniques a wrestler knows and can perform effectively, the more successful he'll be. Thousands of wrestlers and coaches considered my first book the most complete wrestling technique book they'd ever read. Now the best has become better!

Winning Wrestling Moves includes all the latest takedowns, mat wrestling, pinning moves, counters, and freestyle wrestling. This book contains 50% more moves than the original book. We believe it's by far the most in-depth, detailed, and complete collection of wrestling moves ever compiled. We included small but important details about the moves, details that can mean the difference between scoring points or getting scored upon. The latest refinements in teaching and executing are included for today's wrestler and coach.

The first chapter covers all of the basic skills you will need to master the other moves. Chapter 2 describes an extensive variety of takedowns, showing you how to initiate them from several different positions and numerous options for finishing the takedowns.

To learn moves for getting away from your opponent, read chapter 3 on escapes and reversals. Chapter 4 then shows you how to take advantage of opportunities for breakdowns and rides, and chapters 4 and 5 explain the varieties of pinning combinations. Finally, chapter 6 shows you how to work freestyle turns into your wrestling technique.

Winning Wrestling Moves will fully prepare you to succeed in wrestling. The techniques explained here are essential. To be the *very* best, however, requires that you perform with great intensity in your practices and matches. So, if you want to get the most out of the information in this book, consider this:

> Most men stop when they begin to tire.
> Good men go until they think they are going to collapse.
> But the VERY BEST know the mind tires before the body and push themselves further and further beyond all limits.
> Only when all these limits are shattered can the unattainable be reached.
>
> —Mark Mysnyk

Acknowledgments

The authors would like to thank the following wrestlers for their help in posing for the pictures: Terry Brands, Tom Brands, Bart Chelesvig, Matt Dickey, Jack Griffin, Kevin Hogan, Mike Hrusha, Kenny Johnson, Matt Nerem, Mike Neuman, Joe Pantaleo, David Ray, Joel Sharratt, Terry Steiner, Troy Steiner, Keith Trammell, Pablo Ubasa, Bill Zadick, and Chad Zaputil.

We would also like to thank Wayne Johnson and Steve Yagla for their efforts and expertise in taking the photographs, and DeAnna Sports and the Steindler Orthopedic Clinic for their help in sponsoring the production of this book. In addition, we want to express our deep gratitude to our wives and families; without their patience and support, this book would never have been completed.

Finally, the authors set out to produce the highest quality wrestling technique book possible, and feel privileged to donate all of the proceeds to Grace Community Church in Coralville, Iowa, to be used in the ministry of our Lord and Savior, Jesus Christ.

Using This Book

This book has been written as if it is directly coaching the wrestler reading it. The wrestler doing the moves described in the text wears the black Iowa wrestling singlet. If a counter to a move is described *immediately after* the move (rather than in a separate section including only counters), the wrestler in the lighter uniform is doing the move described.

For both consistency and clarity, all offensive takedowns are shown attacking the opponent's left side, and the counters for takedowns are shown with the opponent attacking the right side. On the mat, the top wrestler is shown starting on the left. It is extremely important to realize, though, that not only can the moves be done to the other side, but that they should be practiced and mastered to *both* sides to make you a better and more complete wrestler.

Moves marked by a ★ are key moves that all advanced wrestlers should master. Once mastered, they are highly effective for that particular situation. They are not necessarily the most difficult to do but are advanced and probably not appropriate for beginners.

All of the moves have been named to help the reader refer to them. Because some moves have various names, you may know a move by a name different than the one we've used in this book.

The book attempts to list all or nearly all of the possible options from different positions you may get into while wrestling. Because some moves can be used from a variety of positions, they are listed in different locations throughout the book. Due to space constraints, rather than repeat the entire description and picture of the move each time it is used, the text refers you to the page where the move is pictured and described in detail.

Finally, the pictures are taken from the angle that best shows the key points to the move. In some instances, the two wrestlers may be in markedly different positions in sequential pictures, such as facing opposite directions. In most cases it should be obvious that this change of positions is not a part of the move and is done only to highlight the important points.

1
Basic Skills

A basic skill is either a fundamental wrestling technique or a skill that is key to several other moves. In either case, all wrestlers should master these seven basic skills: stance and movement, penetration step, lifting, hip heist, back arch, back step, and coming to a base.

STANCE AND MOVEMENT

Whether you use a staggered or a square stance, certain key points apply. Most of your weight should be on the balls of your feet, as shown, *not* on your heels. To move forward or shoot or to back up or sprawl, you must be on the balls of your feet. Being on your heels means you have to shift your weight, and even that short time may be the difference between success and failure. Stay on the balls of your feet when you move; take short steps, and never cross your legs. Your knees should be comfortably bent and your body flexed forward slightly at the waist (too far forward and it is easy for your opponent to snap you down). Your elbows stay close to your side to protect you from your opponent's offensive attack, and your hands should remain in front so you can stop your opponent if he shoots in.

PENETRATION STEP

The penetration step, with slight variations, is the basic initial step used to penetrate during takedowns. Leading with either leg, take a big forward step with the lead foot and push off the trail foot (see "Penetration Step," p. 5). Don't "wind up" by leaning back before you shoot in—this telegraphs your shot. Your head should be up and your back straight. Keep your chest (and therefore your weight) over your lead leg. If your lead foot is too far in front of your chest, you will be open for a pancake (see pages 13, 92–93).

If you can penetrate deeply enough without hitting the mat with the knee of your trail leg, that's fine. Otherwise, hit down on that knee and bounce right up. Don't slide on that knee, and don't go down to your other knee. The surest and easiest finishes to singles, doubles, and high crotches are from the standing position, so the penetration step should ideally get you in and right up, not just in and then stuck underneath the opponent on your knees. If you are practicing the penetration step by yourself, come back up to a good stance after each shot and keep your elbows in close to your body throughout the entire move (to prevent the opponent from underhooking your arms).

LIFTING

No matter what position you are lifting a man from—in front, behind, on the side, or down on the mat—lift with your legs, not your back. Your hips and legs are the strongest part of your body, and to use them maximally you need your hips underneath you, with your back straight, or nearly so, as shown.

★ HIP HEIST

In the hip heist the hips are lifted, or hoisted, off the mat and then rapidly and powerfully turned. The move can be used as an escape from almost all positions. The following description is from the referee's position, but from a sit-out, a switch, or a stand-up at any level, the basic action is the same. You want to get as far from your opponent as possible, so the first move is a big step with your outside (right) foot at approximately a 45-degree angle. This extends the top man and weakens his grip around your waist. Next, kick your left leg forward, just as in a long sit-out (a), and while that leg is still in the air, kick the right leg straight out (b). Before either leg hits, you should turn toward the outside by whipping your right elbow down (this elbow action not only helps you turn, but if his arm is around your waist, it also helps break his grip) and throwing your left leg over your right leg.

a

b

★ BACK ARCH

The back arch involves arching backward (from your feet to your head or shoulder). This movement is used in several throws, especially freestyle throws. The back arch can be used in front of, in back of, or on the side of the opponent. The following describes the move in front of the opponent: Your hips are the key; first, get them in tight to the opponent, and then explode with them for power. To get the hips in tight, step your left foot to the outside of his right foot, then step up between his feet with your right leg (a). You will end up straddling his right foot. You could also reverse your steps, first stepping between his legs with your right foot and then to the outside of his right foot with your left foot. When stepping, bend your knees so your hips are below his. Next, explode your hips into him and arch back (b). This should send his legs flying in the air. Keep the arch through the entire move, look straight back over your head, land on top of your head or left shoulder, and then turn. Do not tuck your chin. This takes away your arch and forces you to land on the back of your head, which will hurt! As you are arching back, bend your knees slightly forward to take some of the weight off your head. If you bend them too much, your weight will shift toward your feet, causing you to lose your arch.

a

b

This move can be practiced in five different stages:

1. Stand with your back about 2 to 3 feet from a wall, arch back, and walk down the wall with your hands. Touch your head, then walk back up the wall. Then move 6 inches closer to the wall and repeat the same action. The closer you stand to the wall the more you have to arch.
2. Grab a partner's hand and step between his feet with one foot and on the outside of his feet with the other foot. Then explode your hips in and arch back. Have your partner control your descent and then also pull you up after your head hits.
3. Repeat all the key steps from #2 but now without a partner. Step in, explode your hips, arch back, hit on top of your head, and then turn to your base.
4. Use a throw dummy. This can help build your confidence since your head doesn't have to hit at all.
5. Drill an actual throw with a partner.

★ BACKSTEP

The backstep is the basic foot and hip motion used when doing hip tosses and arm and shoulder throws. Begin by stepping your right foot across to the opponent's right foot. Don't step too much past his foot because this will extend you and take away your power. Then step your left foot up so that the toes touch the outside heel of your right foot. Bend your knees so that your hips are lower than your opponent's. Once you've reached this position, don't take more steps. Rise on the balls of both feet and pivot on them (a). You should end up with both feet parallel and pointing in the opposite direction they started. They shouldn't be any more than 6 to 8 inches apart, and your knees should still be bent. Your hips should be completely through. This is the key to the move. If you led with your right foot, you should end up with your left hip outside his right hip. Once you've reached this position, straighten your legs to lift your opponent's weight off his feet (b) and then finish the throw.

a

b

COMING TO A BASE

Coming to a base refers to getting up from flat on your belly to your hands and knees. The correct way of getting to your base after you've been broken flat onto the mat is to bring one knee up to your side and then to push back over that knee, as shown below. Keep your elbows close to your knees to block the opponent from putting in a leg ride.

An incorrect but unfortunately common method of coming to a base is to simply push up with your hands first and then trying to bring your knees underneath you. This method spends a lot of energy, is ineffective against a good wrestler, and makes it easy for your opponent to put in an arm bar.

2
Takedowns

There is probably greater variety in takedowns than in any other aspect of wrestling. Takedowns can be initiated from several different positions: from any of a number of tie-ups, without a tie-up at all, as a second or third move in a chain of takedown attempts, or as a counter to your opponent's move. A takedown attacks an opponent's upper or lower body, or both. Once the takedown has been initiated, it can be finished in numerous ways. A successful wrestler is aware of these options and reflexively uses the right one depending on the situation.

DOUBLE-LEG TAKEDOWN

As you can guess from the name, when doing a double-leg takedown you grab both of your opponent's legs.

Penetration Step

You can penetrate by stepping either between your opponent's legs or to the outside of them. If stepping between them, step your left foot at least as deep as both of his feet and move your head just to the outside of his left hip, as shown below. Your shoulders should always be over your lead knee as you shoot in. For further penetration, keep driving into your opponent and go down to your left knee, stepping your right foot up to the outside of his left foot. Ideally, you will lift him or finish right away. There are finishes you can do when you get stuck underneath him, but it's usually best to spend the least amount of time possible on your knees.

Snatch Double Leg

It's possible to get a double leg without hitting either knee. Once you are close to your opponent, bend your knees to lower your hips, drive in with your head on either side and your shoulder in his gut, and grab behind both his knees, as shown. Continue to drive into him and pull both of his feet off the mat.

FINISHES FROM DOWN ON THE MAT

The basic position: You are on both knees, your head is to one side of your opponent's hips, and your arms are controlling him either at his knees (this is best; see photo) or at his hip. Rather than controlling your opponent's thighs, you want to control him at a level that bends. This takes his power away and makes it easier to control him. With each of the finishes from on the mat, your knees have to be underneath your upper body (you can't be sprawled forward).

Hooking His Leg

If you lead with your left leg, drive through your opponent so that you go down on your left knee. Next, step up with your right foot, hook his leg, and drive through him, as shown.

Cutting His Knee

Chop the outside of your opponent's left knee with your right arm while coming up on your left foot and driving into him, as shown. Use your head to help drive him over.

Sweeping His Knee

If you led with your outside (right) leg and penetrated deeply, your right foot will be at the level of your opponent's left foot, and your left knee will be down on the mat. Do not stop here, but as a continuous move drive across your opponent by stepping up your left leg so that your left foot and knee are just to the outside of his right foot and knee (a). From here use your left knee to "sweep" his knee and leg and continue to drive over that leg (b).

a

b

Duckunder

As you try to pull the opponent's knees into you, he will try to sprawl his hips back (p. 6, page top). As he does, let go of his right thigh with your left arm and change to a high crotch position, as shown. As you do this, throw your head back to help move his arm and body past you.

Taking Him With Your Head

Lift the opponent's feet off the mat or at least lift him enough so that most of his weight is off his feet. Pull down and in on his right leg, lift his left leg higher, and use your head to drive him to the mat, as shown.

Taking Him Over Your Head

If your opponent was able to sprawl his right leg back but you still have control of his right hip and left knee, chop down on his left knee, duck your head, and throw your left arm hard to take him over your head, as shown. This move must be done explosively, and you must buckle your opponent's left leg; otherwise he will be in a position to wizzer you with his right arm.

Catching His Elbow Around Your Waist

If your opponent puts one or both hands around your waist, the roll as described in the single-leg section (pp. 25–26) can be done.

Head Between His Legs

If your head gets stuck on the mat between your opponent's legs, you can change to a single or bring your knees up under you enough so you can lift him (a). There are two finishes you can do from this position. First, you can change your grip on his right knee so that you are under it and can pop that leg up over your head. At the same time, pull down on his left thigh, duck and turn your head toward his left thigh, and turn toward him (b). Second, you can throw your left arm around his left thigh (c) and slide out behind him.

In many of these moves just described, your opponent will frequently be trying to grab one or both of your ankles. That makes each one of those moves more difficult, but certainly not impossible, and you should still be able to do them.

a

b

c

STANDING FINISHES

You can get to this basic position from the single leg (page 21, photo *c*) or following a duckunder. You control your opponent's left knee with your right arm, and your left arm is around his right waist or hip while his right foot is on the mat.

★Knee Sweep

You want to lift the opponent's left knee while stepping your left leg so that your left knee is on the outside of his right knee. Do not step and plant your foot, instead sweep his knee with yours (your leg will be bent, and your knee will be sweeping just at or above his knee, as shown in the photo). When you pull your opponent's left knee to the outside, also lift it, getting weight off of his right foot and making it easier to sweep his knee. As you sweep his knee, use your left arm to pull him down in a circular motion. Thus, there are three key movements: lifting your opponent's leg through the whole move, sweeping his knee (your aim is to block and sweep, not hook and trip), and pulling him down in a circular motion with waist or hip control.

Ankle Sweep

This is the same basic movement as the knee sweep, but instead of sweeping the opponent's leg with your knee, sweep his ankle with your foot. As with the knee sweep, don't hook his leg with yours (it is not a trip). Also, lift his other leg and pull down around his waist as you sweep him.

Inside Trip

Use both of your arms to lift your opponent and get some weight off of his planted (right) foot. At the same time, step your left leg behind his knee, as shown, and drive your shoulder into his chest or stomach as you sweep his leg toward you and off the mat.

Dump

This move can be done with the opponent's leg between or to the outside of your legs. Slide step toward his right leg (take a short step toward his right leg with your left foot), then take a big backward and circular step with your right foot (see photo). Put pressure down on the opponent's left thigh with your chest and use your waist control to bring him to the mat.

Double-Leg Tackle

If the opponent can sprawl and get both his legs back to the mat, do not wait until he is sprawled completely away and you have lost all control. Instead, use his momentum to drive into him, lock your hands around his legs at knee level, pull his knees together, and take him down to the mat in one smooth motion.

The move from this position is the same as from the feet off the mat position described below in the Turk move.

FINISHES WITH OPPONENT'S FEET OFF THE MAT

You can get to this basic position by lifting after getting to the penetration level. Your arms are controlling your opponent's hips or thighs and you have his feet off the mat, as shown.

★Turk

A *Turk* is a move that uses one of your legs to hook an opponent's leg above his knee. The origin of the name is uncertain. This is one of the first finishes you should be considering, since it takes the opponent to his back in a hold that's tough to get out of. Lift his left leg so that you can step across him with your right leg and hook above his right knee (a). Drive through him and as you hit the mat, land with your weight on him, your head slightly off to the side, and your right arm posted so you don't roll through (b). You can then adjust by hooking his near shoulder and driving your elbow to his ear or by throwing in a half nelson.

a

b

Taking Him With Your Head

Swing both of your opponent's legs high to the same side your head is on to clear his legs (a). When his legs are at their high point, change your arms so that your right arm is around his right (lower) leg and your left arm is controlling his waist (b). Drop down to your right knee, leaving your left knee up. Set his hip on your left knee, keep control of his right leg with your arm, and put a half nelson on him with your left arm (c). All that's left is to take him to the mat. He still has his right arm to post with, and although you could probably drive him over it, the finish is more effective if you eliminate his post by circling him toward the front as you take him to the mat.

If you can swing your opponent's legs high enough so he can't get his right leg down as a post, you don't need to change your hand control (as shown in *b*); instead, set him on your left knee and finish as just described.

a

b

c

Taking the Man Over Your Head

Your left arm is going to throw the opponent over your head. To do so, drive that arm up hard from his hip to under his arm and keep driving over your head. At the same time, duck your head to the outside (so he will slide off of it easier), pull down on his left hip, and step backward with your right leg, as shown.

Bear Hug

Bring your right arm up from around the opponent's thigh to lock hands with your other arm around his lower back. Do this explosively because when you release his thigh, he will probably be sprawling in an attempt to get out. With the bear hug, you should be able to "crunch" him directly down to his back.

COUNTERS TO DOUBLE LEGS

Sprawl

The first counter to a double leg is blocking the opponent's penetration with your arms and sprawling your legs back; this prevents him from getting control of your legs, and possibly sets up a takedown of your own.

Square Your Hips

Probably the best counter to a double leg once the opponent has your legs is to square your hips and arch them into him. Do not lay your chest on his back with no hip pressure at all (a). The object of sprawling is to get your legs back and your hip into his head and shoulder, putting pressure on him (b). Many wrestlers make the mistake of sprawling hard at first, then relaxing and letting the opponent pull his legs back in after the initial counter. You must keep steady pressure on your opponent and realize you are fighting with the strongest part of your body (hips and legs) against a weaker part of his body (arms), so you should be able to win this battle.

a

b

Pancake

If the opponent shoots in with his arms out, he is open for a pancake. The details of this move are explained in the short offense section (pp. 92–93). If his head is coming in to your right side, underhook his right arm with your left arm and overhook his left arm with your right arm, as shown. If you underhook the same side his head is on, it's easier for him to get his head under your arm and spin through (page 93, photo *c*). Step to the side and use his forward momentum and your arms to flip him to his back. You essentially flip him like a pancake and he ends up flat.

Cross Face

If possible, when an opponent tries a move, do not merely counter it and end up in a neutral position, but score a takedown yourself. A cross face can help to both free your legs and get around behind him for a takedown. A cross face involves placing your arm across your opponent's face and on his far arm. This turns his head away from you. At the same time, continue to sprawl your legs back and spin around to the back of him, trying to grab either his near or far ankle with your hand or hook his near ankle with your foot (page 41).

Chest Squeeze

If you are having trouble getting your legs free when the opponent's head is to the outside or between your legs, you can reach around his chest, not around his waist where he could roll you (pp. 25–26), and lock your hands palm to palm. From this position, continue to arch your hips into the opponent while pulling up on his chest, as shown.

Roll

If your opponent has penetrated deeply, you can lock your hands by reaching around his waist with your right arm and around his right thigh with your left arm (a). Keep his right shoulder blocked so that he can't pop it out. Draw your right thigh into him and roll over (b), either releasing him as you roll (if it is freestyle and you want to get tilt points) or getting on top of him with control.

a

b

HIGH SINGLE-LEG TAKEDOWN

Also called the *high leg single.* This move involves attacking only one leg.

With a deep penetration step (and hitting down on one knee at least momentarily), you end up locked around your opponent's knee. Lock your hands behind his knee, not above or below it. Grip your hands together palm-to-palm with your outside hand on top (a). Your opponent will only be able to grab your inside (left) wrist, and if he tries to pull it up to break your grip, he will be pulling it directly into your other hand. He should not be able to break your grip. However, if you lock your hands with your inside hand on top, the only thing keeping him from pulling your hands apart will be the fingertips of your right hand. He can easily break this grip.

You should be on your toes, able to move, and. your head can be in one of two good positions: The first has your head in his ribs (b). This makes it difficult for him to get an effective wizzer on you. The second has your biceps and shoulder on top of his thigh. Apply downward pressure on his thigh as you lift up on his knee.

In the "head in the ribs" position (b), the opponent can grab your inside wrist and possibly rotate it, or grab your elbows and drive his knee down hard to free it. Neither of these can be done if you have your biceps and shoulder on his thigh. However, there is a drawback to that position: When you shoulder is down tight on his thigh, there are some finishes you can't do as well with your head in his side.

If your opponent gets you out of position by jamming your head down (c), throw your right shoulder into him, circle your head away (d), and then get back to either of the two positions just described.

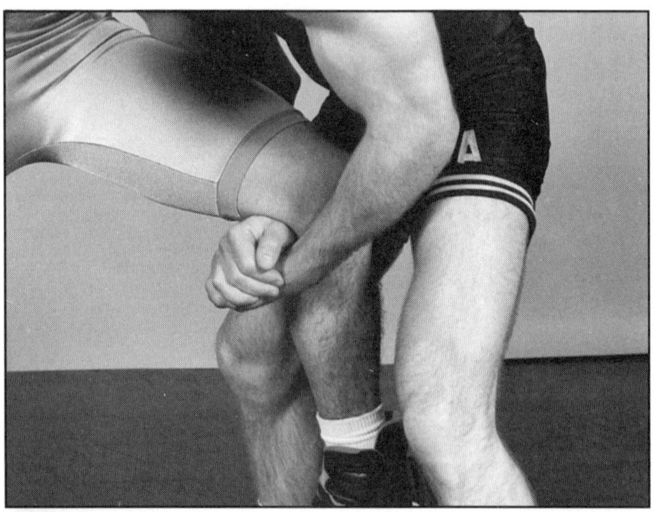

a

b

c

d

Penetration Step

Step with either your outside or inside foot (a), and lead with your inside (left) arm to prevent the wizzer. You have a wizzer on when an opponent has his arm around your leg or back and you overhook that arm with your arm (page 82, photo *a*). He can wizzer only your outside arm, so if you lead with your outside arm, he will be able to sprawl and wizzer your arm before you have a chance to get a good grip on his leg (b). If you lead with your inside arm, you can get good control around his knee with that arm, and then lock up your outside arm (c). He then may be able to get some kind of a wizzer on you, but it won't be that effective.

a

b

c

FINISHES WHEN HIS LEG IS BETWEEN YOURS

★Dump or Run the Pipe

This move gets its name from "dumping" your opponent on his butt, or from the sliding action applied to his leg ("running the pipe"). From a single-leg position with your shoulder on top of his thigh, take a short step in front of him with your left foot (a, next page), then a longer, backward step with your right foot as you continue to keep pressure down on his thigh (b, next page). It is important to keep your shoulder tight on his thigh. If your head and shoulder are slipping to the outside, it will be difficult to finish.

Dump Variant

A variation of the dump is to pinch your opponent's legs between yours, reach behind your butt and grab his foot, then dump him as previously described.

Reacting to the Counters to the Dump

If you attempt either the Dump or the Dump Variant and your opponent counters by pulling his leg back, you can finish with a Barsagar. This move is described in more detail later (page 22).

a

b

Block His Opposite Knee in Front

If your opponent turns away from you, resulting in his left leg rotating inward and his right foot pointing away, his knee can bend when you try to put pressure on his thigh (a), making it hard to dump him. However, that opens him up for another finish: Use your right arm to block in front of his thigh (b), use your right shoulder to put pressure in the back of his left thigh, then circle behind him to bring him down to the mat. The counter to the knee block is to turn into your opponent, which opens him up for a dump. Thus, you can use the knee block to set up the dump or vice versa.

Leg Sweep

If you can't get him down by blocking in front of his thigh, you can pull his leg out by changing your right arm to around his left thigh and your left hand to his ankle. As you pull his leg up in front of you, use your right foot to sweep his right leg (c).

a

b

c

Block His Knee in Back

You can use your left arm to block behind your opponent's right knee and then circle in front of him, as shown.

Leg Hook and Thigh Block

A variation of Blocking His Knee in Back is to use your right foot and leg to hook his left leg, then shift your right hand to around his left thigh and your left hand to behind his right thigh. From here, drive straight into him to finish the move.

Change to a Double

Pull the opponent toward you so that he must hop his foot toward you. As he hops, drive into him and step your right foot as far behind him as possible, then change to a double-leg takedown and drive him to the mat.

★Sit Back

This finish works best when the opponent has his weight forward, especially if he has a wizzer and is driving you forward. Unlock your hand from around his knee and slide your right hand up to his crotch. Next, step your right foot across to the front of his right foot, sit down on your right hip, and use your head to drive his chest or stomach back, as shown. As soon as you hit, come up on top of him.

Hooking and Lifting His Leg

Head in Front

Hook your opponent's left leg with your right leg, release your hands from around his left knee, and reach for his right leg (a). Then drive into him with your head in his ribs. Lift his leg with your right leg throughout the move.

Head in Back

If your opponent counters your initial single leg by pushing your head to the outside, use your left leg to hook his leg (b) and finish by driving through him.

a

b

Barsagar

The Barsagar is easiest to do when the opponent's leg is to the outside of yours. The Barsagar can be done when the opponent's leg is between yours, but it requires that you clear his left leg to the outside of your right leg first. This can be done in a continuous move by stepping your right leg back to clear the opponent's left foot, pulling his left knee up onto your right hip, and then finishing the move. The movement is described in detail on page 22.

Lifting His Leg Up

This can be done in one smooth motion by stepping your left leg out and back while lifting the opponent's leg (a). As soon as your leg is behind his leg, step it in and underneath his leg and set it on your hip. Your leg moves in a continuous motion—out, back, and then in again under his leg.

This move can also be done in stages. You can pinch your opponent's leg between your legs, then unlock your hands and reach down between your legs to his heel (b). After you have controlled his heel, step your inside leg out, back (c), and then under his leg. At the same time lift his leg so that when you step your leg back under his, his leg is up on your thigh.

Whether you lift his leg in one motion or in the steps just outlined, hold the opponent's heel and use your forearm to cover his toes and twist his foot out (d). If you don't have his foot controlled this way, he can easily kick out (page 35).

a

b

c

d

Finishes Once His Leg Is Up

Once you have your opponent's leg up, there are several ways to finish:

Trip Forward

Use your right leg to trip above his knee and drive him forward (a).

Trip Backward

This is actually more of a block than a trip. Step your left foot toward the front so that your opponent must hop backward to keep his balance. At the same time you are stepping with your left foot, use your right foot to block his ankle so that he can't follow you (b). Before you circle, release your right hand from his knee and change it to an underhook. Then, when you circle and block, pull down on his shoulder.

Leg Lift

This move can be done two ways. The first is a continuation of clearing your opponent's leg to the inside (page 18, photo *a*). Instead of lifting his leg only enough to get it on your hip, lift it as high as you can so that his other foot comes off the mat. The second way is starting with knee and ankle control. Lift his leg as high as possible, and at the same time take a big step away from him with your left foot. This extends him and makes it easier to get him off the mat (c).

a

b

c

Knee Pressure

Grab just above your opponent's knee and around the inside of it as far as possible, then twist his knee and ankle out while pulling down his leg (d). You can also step your left foot in front of him toward his right foot, just as in a dump, to help take him to the mat.

Both Arms Under His Leg

The last three finishes can also be done when both of your arms are underneath your opponent's leg. To get into this position (once you have reached the knee and heel position), use your knee to lift and hold his leg (e), then change your hand from over to under his ankle (f). It is important to use your left knee for control because if you try to hold his leg only with your right arm while you switch your left arm from over to under his ankle, he can easily power his leg down to the mat.

With both arms under your opponent's leg, you can raise his leg higher; but he can turn away and kick free easier since you don't have the heel trapped as well as in the other position.

Cradle

Lift your opponent's leg high so it is near his head. Some opponents will lean forward, doing you a favor by bringing their head closer to their knee. If they do, change your right arm to around his head while sliding your left arm up from his ankle to under his knee and lock up the cradle (g). Then circle him backward to the mat.

d

e

f

g

FINISHES WHEN HIS LEG IS TO THE OUTSIDE OF YOURS

You may end up in this position two ways: Either you can intentionally put your opponent's leg to the outside or he may do it. Some opponents prefer to put their leg to the outside, and others will put their foot to the outside but keep their knee to the inside to block you (a). If he blocks with his knee, lift his leg so that it is on your hip (b). If he is still able to block your chest with his knee, unlock your hands briefly to use your inside hand to knock his knee to the outside of your hip, then relock your hands. If he keeps his leg between your legs but you want it outside, step your outside leg out and back as you throw his leg to the outside and step your hip back underneath his leg (c).

b

c

Once his leg is to the outside of yours, you can do any of the following finishes.

Change to a Double

Lift your opponent's knee to the outside with your right arm (*c*, above). Then step in and reach around his waist with your left arm. From this position, use any of the finishes described for the double leg from the standing level (pp. 9–10).

★Barsagar

The name for this move comes from an Iranian wrestler in the 1970s who used the move quite effectively. Another name for it is a *far knee block*. Lift the opponent's left knee so that it is up on your thigh. At the same time, drive into him by stepping across with your left foot and reach with your left hand to the outside of his right knee (a). Do not try to chop his knee, just block it. Continue to drive into the opponent to force him over his right leg. You get additional force by throwing his left leg over (b). You should still be on your feet when he goes down to the mat because if you stay tight with him as he is going down, you could easily get rolled. However, as soon as he hits the mat, be aggressive in covering him.

a

b

Heave-Ho

This move is so called because you lift the opponent's leg as high off the mat as you can. Put inward pressure on his knee to get him to react and push it out. When he does, throw his leg out and up as high as you can. Step your right leg slightly back at the same time so that his right leg won't hit it on the way up. Bring his other leg completely off the mat so that he goes down to the mat on his hands, as shown.

Heave-Ho to a Turk

If you can't get your opponent's left leg up high enough to get his right leg off the mat, clear it enough so that you can step into a Turk, similar to the double-leg finish (pp. 10–11).

Head Chop

Block the inside of your opponent's right ankle with your right foot while unlocking your hands and using your left arm to "club" the right side of his head, as shown. Also, rotate your hips to the right, pull his left leg back, and take him backward in a circular motion.

Blocking in Front of His Far Ankle

If you attempt the head chop but can't get the opponent down, hook your left hand around his head and use your left leg to block the outside of his right ankle. Then, pull down on his head, lift up on his left knee, and continue to block with your foot, as shown. The head chop can be used to set up this move and vice versa.

Leg Sweep

Lift the opponent's left knee to get most of the weight off his right foot. In the same motion, use your left foot to sweep his right leg off the mat, as shown. Then use downward pressure on his right knee to take him to the mat.

Dropping Underneath Him

If your opponent is pushing down on your head (a), drop down and post on your left knee and left arm. As you do this, lift his left leg and drive your head underneath it (b). From here, turn toward his left leg and come out behind him.

a

b

Change to Knee and Ankle Control

If your opponent is driving your head down, another option is to grab his heel with your left hand, turn and move your head away from him so that his downward pressure becomes sideways pressure, and then lift his heel and finish with the heel and knee control shown on page 18.

Dump

Do this move as described when the opponent's leg was on the inside (pp. 15–16).

FINISHES WHEN HIS LEG IS ON THE MAT

Lace His Leg

As the opponent is driving his leg back, instead of keeping your hands locked around his knee, cup your right hand around his knee and post on your left hand (a). If you have a secure hold around his knee, the force of his own sprawl frequently lifts his leg up. If it doesn't, continue to drive into your opponent, stepping your knees underneath you and your head under him (b). From here finish with any of the finishes described on page 8.

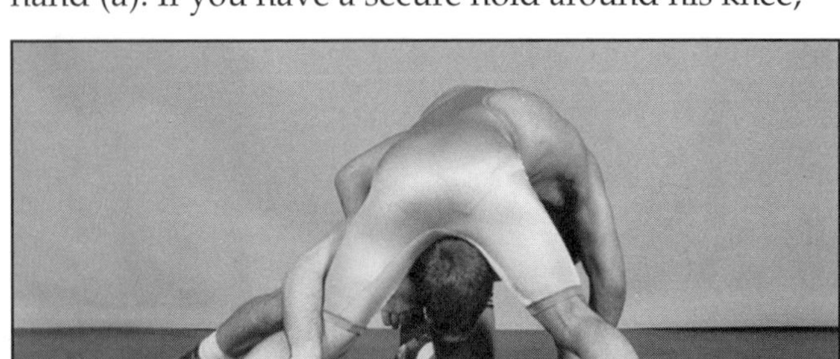

a

b

Spin to Your Feet

Rather than keeping your hands locked behind his knee, turn your right hand down so that your right palm is on the mat and your left hand is on top of your right hand. If it feels more comfortable, your left hand may be on bottom. Then, raise up on your toes, get your butt up, and spin toward the back of your opponent, as shown. He will usually come up to his feet as you spin so that you end up in a standing single-leg position.

Spin and Block

If you want to keep the opponent from spinning with you, put your right forearm and elbow down on the mat on the inside of his left leg, as shown. Then spin behind him and try to hook his left ankle with your right leg.

High Crotch

If your opponent is sprawling back with his hips squared up to you, raise your right knee up and slide your left knee under his left knee. At the same time use your right arm to throw him behind you, and your left arm to hit a high crotch, as shown.

★Roll

An incorrect reaction to a single-leg shot is to reach around the opponent's waist. If an opponent does this, keep your right arm around his leg and use your left hand to grab his left wrist. Sit your legs under you, pull his arm tight, and lift your head to throw him over (a, next page). You cannot slowly reach for his wrist, methodically get control of it, and then hit the move because he will pull his wrist away and adjust his weight to prevent the move. You must hit it quickly and explosively, usually just after you shoot. Once you have completed the move, hold your opponent there long enough to get back points (b, next page), then step your left leg over your right leg and turn toward his legs.

a

b

LOW SINGLE LEG

Penetration

The penetration step is the same as for the high single leg but instead of reaching for your opponent's knee, reach for his ankle as you are down momentarily on both knees. As with the high single leg, lead with your inside arm and do not bring your outside arm around his leg until after you have penetrated.

Finishes

Cup His Heel

You can finish by cupping the opponent's heel so that he can't sprawl back and driving straight through him (a).

Spin

Or you can post your hands, spin, and come around him (b). (Shoot in straight and then spin. Don't shoot off to the side as you penetrate.)

a

b

Finishes From Behind Him

Turn the corner, grab above the opponent's left knee with your right arm, and drive your right shoulder into his thigh (a).

Grab Far Ankle

Always look for the opponent's right ankle. If you turn the corner and he leaves the right ankle close enough, grab it and drive over it.

Blocking His Knee

Reach across with your right arm to the front of his opposite knee and drive him forward (b).

a

b

SET-UPS FOR HIGH AND LOW SINGLE LEGS

The purpose of a set-up is to get closer to the leg you are shooting for and to clear one or both of the opponent's arms so he can't block you. In general, you can set up your opponent by moving him (with or without a tie-up), such as circling away from the leg you want to shoot for, making him step that leg toward you. Or, you can use a tie-up, which is one of several ways to grab or control your opponent's arms, head, or body when you're in the neutral position. A tie-up can give you the control to clear his arms or to move him to bring his leg toward you. Finally, you can fake one shot and use his reaction to that shot to set up the single leg.

SET-UPS FROM TIE-UPS

Wrist Control

A common tie-up for the single leg and other takedowns is to start with wrist control. The most common way to grab the opponent's wrist is with your palm facing inside with your thumb on top (a).

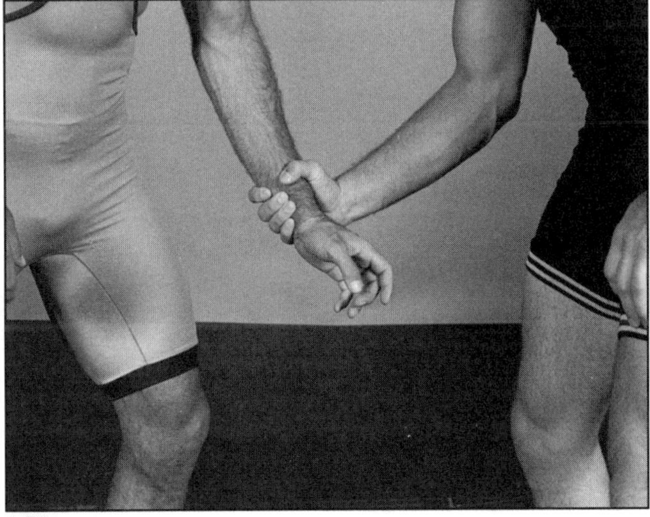

a

This feels natural and can be very effective, but unless you have a very strong grip he can break your control simply by rotating his hand out (b). A more effective way to grab his wrist is with your palm facing out and your thumb on the bottom (c). It is much more difficult to break this grip.

Drive His Arm Out

With wrist control clear your opponent's arm. Then lead with your left arm to grab his left leg (d). You do not need to release his right wrist until you have control of his leg with your left arm.

Drive His Arm Into Him

You can also eliminate the opponent's left arm from stopping your penetration by driving it directly toward and then behind his leg.

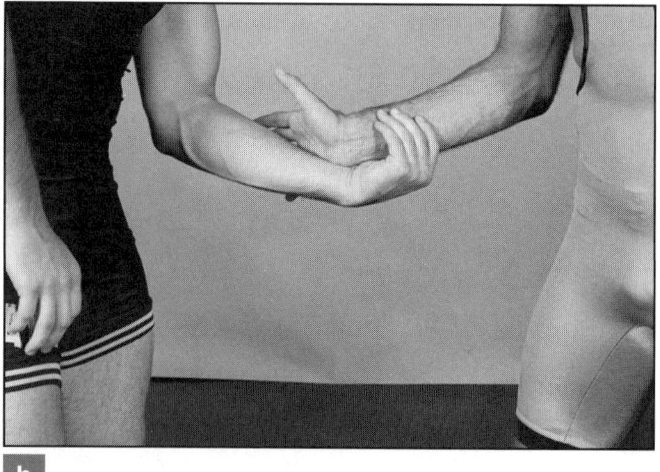

b

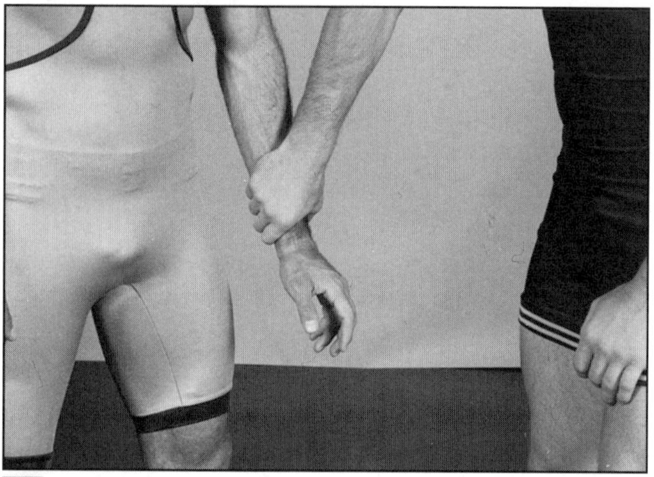

c

d

Double Wrist Tie-Up

Another wrist tie-up that makes it easier to drive your opponent's arm into him is to grab his wrist with both hands, like gripping a baseball bat (a). Drive his arm into his leg, then release his arm and get control of his left leg. If the opponent steps this left leg back, step your left leg across him and sweep his arm through hard (b). Clear your left leg out of the way as you sweep him by. You may be able to snatch his leg as it goes by you or possibly snap him down to the mat .

a

b

Pop, Chop, or Drag

Pop

As your opponent is reaching for you or after he has placed his hand on your shoulder, pop his arm (or arms) above his elbow to clear his arm. Reach with your left arm at the same time. If you pop him below his elbow, his arm can bend and he may still be able to block you.

Chop

As your opponent is reaching for you, you can also chop his arms down. If he is anchored solidly on your shoulder and you can't clear him, move your shoulders back quickly to loosen his grip just before you chop him.

Drag

Reach across with your left arm to grab your opponent's left arm above the elbow (page 83, photo *a*). You don't need to drag him completely by you, just enough to expose his side so you can shoot in on him.

Fighting for Inside Control

"Inside control" means controlling your opponent's arms with your elbow and forearm inside of his elbow and forearm. If you are fighting for inside control, as he comes to the inside slide your hand down to his elbow, then drive it up or across him (a) to clear his leg.

He Blocks Your Inside Control

If you have inside control and your opponent comes over your forearm, reach across with your left arm and grab his wrist (b). Drive into him to get close to his leg and then grab the single.

Snap

Snap his head down; then when he reacts and pulls it up, shoot in. As you shoot, you may have to pop his arms up to clear them.

a

b

SET-UPS FROM FAKE SHOTS

Fake to One Leg and Shoot to the Other One

Take a quarter step toward the opponent's right leg, which should be enough to get him to step that leg back and leave the left leg out for you to shoot in on.

Underhook and Wrist Control

With an underhook using your right arm, and wrist control with your left arm, drive the opponent's right wrist toward his right leg as if you are trying to block his knee. If he doesn't step the right leg back, drive over his knee (see *Knee Pick*, page 60). If he does step the leg back (see photo, next page), hold his wrist and then drive it toward his left leg. Release your underhook to come down and control his left knee with your right arm. Release his wrist and lock your hands.

Fake Ankle Pick

From an underhook, step your hips in as if going for an ankle pick (page 58), then when your opponent squares up in front of you, hit a single leg or high crotch.

Fake Drag

Fake drag to one side to get him to sprawl that leg back and then shoot in on the other side.

Fake Snatch Single

Go for any of the snatch singles to one side (discussed below). If you miss it, it is usually because he stepped his leg back and left the other one out. That side should be open for a single or high crotch.

SNATCH SINGLE LEG

In the snatch single, initial control is gained by snatching with your hands behind the opponent's knee (see photo). You get his weight off one leg and grab behind his knee without going down to your knees. Since you need to get only your fingers behind his knee rather than your arm, you do not need to penetrate as far as with a high leg single. Rather than "shooting," or taking a big penetration step, you need only a small step, and you never go down to either knee. The different set-ups will shift the opponent's weight off the leg you are attacking, so you will be able to easily lift his leg off the mat. As you pick his leg up, you want him to be hopping on his right foot with all his weight there so he cannot shift his weight to free his left foot. This is done by moving him—either driving into him or backing away from him. You should be on your toes, not your heels. It only has to be a few small steps until you can pinch the opponent's left leg between your thighs for temporary control and then adjust your grip to the proper lock. If your set-up and subsequent movement after you have his leg does not shift all of his weight to his right foot, you will not be able to hold his left leg long enough to get the proper grip. This is a continuous movement—as soon as you snatch your opponent's leg, continue to move him so that he has to hop on his right leg, taking all of the weight and pressure off his left leg.

SET-UPS FOR THE SNATCH SINGLE LEG

Change Levels

If you are close enough to your opponent, all you have to do is change levels—bend your knees and drop your hips. Then snatch his lead knee, as shown above. You must time it so that he has his weight shifted to his right foot.

Shoulder Hit

Use one arm to hit (or push) your opponent's left shoulder so that he has to take a step back with his right leg for balance. In so doing, he takes all his weight off his left foot. At the same time, with your left arm reach behind his knee to snatch his leg, as shown. After you have lifted his leg, bring your right arm down to lock your hands around his knee.

Toe Block

Start by faking a head tie-up to get your opponent to raise his arms, and penetrate with your right foot so that you are standing on his left foot. This prevents him from stepping his foot back and allows you to snatch his leg.

Head Shuck

From the head and arm control snap the opponent's head and arm away from his left leg. You are not trying to hook and pull his head, but rather drive it to his right side. To do this, raise your left elbow and rotate your left arm down. This should turn his body and make him step his left leg toward you (a). As soon as you finish driving his head away with your left hand, that arm changes directions and comes back toward his leg. Meet his leg as he is stepping into you. Your right hand can continue to block his arm and you should be able to pick up his left leg with your left hand (b).

a

b

★Shrug

This is similar to the head shuck but is done from a different tie-up. If your opponent has control of your head, reach over his arm and grab his head with your right arm. Then, explosively, shrug your right shoulder up and then drive it into his left arm. Also, use your right forearm to drive his head away (a, next page). At the same time, reach across with your left arm to grab his left arm just above the elbow to help pull his arm across his body (b, next page). As with the shuck, bring your left arm back to catch his left knee as he steps (or sometimes runs) in front of you. If you do the move hard enough you will snap him down to the mat and not have to do the single leg.

Two-on-One

See Two-on-One (pp. 101 and 102).

a

b

COUNTERS TO SINGLES

The previous pages involved the offensive component of single-leg takedowns. The defensive component, or counters, to an opponent's single-leg attacks will now be described. Techniques to prevent your opponent from initiating a shot or countering him as he shoots in will be discussed first. This will be followed by counters to the high single leg while standing, counters to the high single leg down on the mat, counters to the seat belt, and counters to the low single leg.

COUNTERS BEFORE OR AS HE SHOOTS

Head-to-Head Tie-Up

The earliest possible counter to any takedown attempt on your legs is to prevent your opponent from shooting in the first place. A tight head-to-head tie-up eliminates most of an opponent's offense. You or your opponent could do an ankle pick from there, but not much else is possible. But if you have a slim lead near the end of the match, a head-to-head tie-up may be desirable. Since both wrestlers are in the same tie-up, it is not necessarily obvious that you are stalling. In general, though, you only get into trouble when you try to protect the lead, and with the exception of the last few seconds, you should always be aggressive.

Block as He Shoots

The next counter to the single leg is to block your opponent as he shoots. By keeping one arm down in front of you, you can readily use that arm to block him. You may use it to simply stop him, as shown, or to begin a head-snap run-around (page 90).

Lead With Your Opposite Leg

If your opponent shoots to only one side, you can frustrate him by using a staggered stance with the leg he doesn't shoot on out in front. The leg he likes to shoot in on is therefore back away from him. (In general, you want to make your opponent wrestle your style, not vice versa. You should probably adjust your stance only if your offensive takedowns are just as effective from that altered stance position.)

Head-Snap Run-Around

This is an excellent counter to any leg attack and is described on pages 89 and 90 in the Short Offense section.

COUNTERS TO THE HIGH SINGLE LEG ON THE FEET WITH HIS HEAD TO THE INSIDE

Basic Defense

One of the basic things you want to do consistently is get your opponent's head down. Push his head down with your left hand, then cover it with your hips to hold it down, as shown. He is a lot less powerful from that position and he is using more energy than you are since he has to use his lower back to hold you up. With your left hand grab your opponent's right hand. This stops him from doing the Barsagar (page 22), changing to a double, lifting your leg up (page 18), or any other move that requires him to move his right hand. Therefore, by holding his head down and controlling his inside wrist, you limit his mobility, make him use more energy, take away his power, and stop most of his offense.

Trip Him Back

After you get your opponent's head down, hook your right leg behind his left leg. Reach behind his right knee with your left hand, as shown, then hip into him and drive him to his butt.

Ankle Pick

Put your right foot to the outside of your opponent's leg and have your knee above his. Put a wizzer on his left arm with your right arm and grab his right arm with your left hand. Then, hop backward and pull him toward you, causing him to step his right leg toward you. As he steps, let go of his right arm and reach down to his ankle, as shown, and force your knee into his thigh, driving his weight over his ankle.

Near-Leg Block

After you have his head down, grab his right wrist with your left hand. Then reach over his back and underneath his right arm with your right arm and grab your own wrist. Lace your right foot around his left ankle (a), then lift his right arm and pull him over that ankle (b).

a

b

Far-Leg Trip

With your hands locked the same way as the last move, step your right leg across to the outside of his far (right) leg (above his knee, as shown). Drive your weight forward, and lift his leg with yours.

Trip Back

With your leg between your opponent's legs, straighten your knee and hook your right foot behind his right knee. Have a wizzer in with your right arm and hop backward so that you get to his side. Lower your hips by bending your left knee, reach behind his left knee with your left hand, and take him backward, as shown below. By keeping your right leg straight you pry on your opponent's legs—forward on his right leg and back on his left leg. If you bend your right knee, you lose this pressure. You can finish by locking up a cradle with your leg still across him or else by scissoring your leg out and getting perpendicular to him. When using your arm to block the near leg, this move is legal; it is *illegal* to use your left leg to trip him backward.

Knee Tilt

After you have your opponent's head down, reach behind his right knee with your left arm. Pull him into you, crunching him up so his head can't pop out. Squat down, posting on your right hand, then throw him, as shown, over your right leg (which he is still holding). Don't sit on your butt and simply roll him back. You should be able to finish on top of your opponent. This move can also be done if he is on his knees on a single and he brings his inside knee up.

Sag Throw

a

b

If the opponent has his hands locked incorrectly (his inside hand on top), use your right arm to wizzer him, and grab his right wrist with your left hand. Rotate your right hip so that your right leg is on his thigh with your knee to the inside and your foot to the outside (a). Jump up in the air and then thrust your right leg down to break your opponent's grip. As you put your right foot down on the mat, you want to place it to the outside of his left leg so that you block it. At the same time, use your left arm to underhook his right side (b), then finish as described later for the sag throw (page 61). If his hands are locked the right way around your leg, it is usually not possible to break his grip, therefore making it impossible to do the move.

Kick-Out

This move counters the single leg by kicking your leg out of your opponent's control. Your knee must be above his hands in order to kick out. If it is, turn your body and point the toes of your left foot away from him. Then kick your right leg out by driving your knee down toward the mat, as shown. Once your leg is free, turn to face him.

You can set up the kick out by driving or reaching toward the opponent's right knee as if you are going to trip him over it. When he steps that leg back, kick out.

Fake Kick-Out to a Switch

If your opponent has your leg above your knee, fake kick-out to get him to follow you, then turn and drop to your knees and hit a standing switch (page 38).

★Back Roll

Start with your leg between your opponent's legs and use your right arm to wizzer his left arm. Grab his left wrist with your left hand. Try to step your left leg down so that he will resist and pull it up. Then step your left leg between his legs and roll over on your back (a and b). Finish by keeping the wizzer with your right arm, using your right foot to hook under your opponent's right leg, and your left arm can either hook his left leg behind the knee or keep control of his wrist. Be aware of where your back is so that you don't pin yourself.

a

b

Stiff Leg

A strictly defensive counter you can do is to straighten your knee and place your foot in your opponent's stomach, using your hands to hold him away so he can't grab your leg above the knee (a). The best time to get into this is when he is coming to his feet with your leg.

Counter to the Stiff Leg

Reach your outside arm around the outside of the opponent's ankle and grab the inside of his foot (b), then turn it in to make him turn away.

a

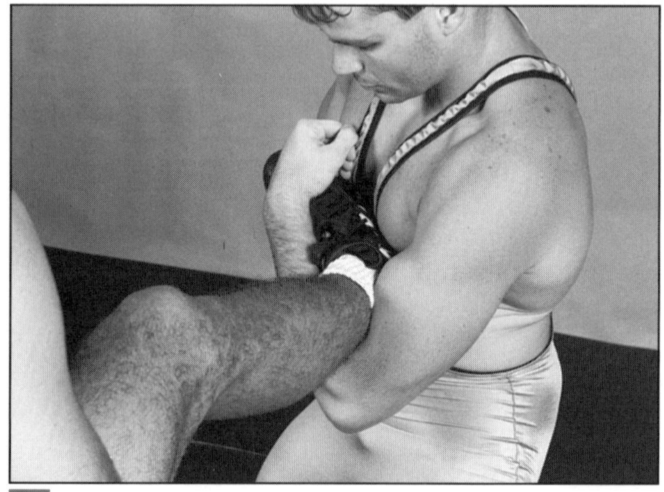

b

COUNTERS TO THE HIGH SINGLE LEG ON THE FEET WITH HIS HEAD TO THE OUTSIDE

When both wrestlers are on their feet, either wrestler may prefer to put his head to the outside. In either case, you must watch out for your opponent changing to a double leg (page 49). Several counters can be done with the opponent's head to the outside, including the *Circle Behind*, the *Arm Drag*, and the *Switch*.

Circle Behind

As you are blocking your opponent's right arm (so that he cannot change to a double) (a), you can circle around behind him. Once you have an angle on him and he can no longer change to a double, you can either reach around his waist (b), or around his left thigh, and then take him to the mat.

a

b

Arm Drag

Use your left arm to keep your opponent from changing to a double, but bring your right arm between his head and your body and hook his right arm (a). From here, simply do an arm drag, turning your hips as you go down so that he lands flat and you land on top of him or on your right hip (b), not on your butt.

a

b

Switch

With your right arm, reach over your opponent's right arm and under his right leg, as shown. Hit a switch just as you would if you were down on the mat.

COUNTERS TO HIGH SINGLE LEG DOWN ON THE MAT WITH HIS HEAD TO THE INSIDE

Sprawl/Hip Pressure

You always want to square your hips to the opponent (a). Initially, you may counter with a wizzer and this means turning your hip into him, but after you've sprawled back, it is probably best to square your hips to him. If you can get enough hip pressure, you can break his grip and counter his shot with the sprawl. To do so, you need to walk your feet back and arch your hips into his head and shoulder. If this does not break your opponent's grip, turn your right hip into his shoulder by scissoring your left leg over your right leg (b). This should drive his shoulder down to the mat and break his grip (c). You can do this only if you have him extended enough so that he doesn't have much power in his shoulders or arms. Once you break his grip, spin around behind him for the takedown.

a

b

c

Grab His Right Wrist

Once you've sprawled back, you may be able to reach under your opponent's chest with your right arm and grab his right wrist. If so, pull it off your leg, keep control of it, and spin around his right side (since he cannot block you).

Grab His Right Arm

Alternatively, you can reach behind both of your opponent's arms with your right arm and grab his right arm, as shown. Use your left arm to grab his right wrist or elbow to help free your leg, and then finish as in the previous move.

★ Step Over His Back

If you've grabbed your opponent's right arm as in the previous move, and you cannot break his grip, sprawl back as far as you can to get him stretched out and circle toward his left side (a). Keep pulling his right arm so that his head and shoulder stay down, then step your right leg (the one he is holding) over his back (b). This will take him to his back.

a

b

Quarter Nelson

Have your left hand on your opponent's head, pushing it down. With your right arm have a wizzer and grab your left wrist. From here, push down on his head, pry up on his left arm, and take him over to his back (a). The move is more effective if instead of pushing down on his head, you can grab his chin with your left hand (b).

a

b

Headlock or Pancake

Push down on your opponent's head with the quarter nelson as in the previous move, then when he reacts by driving his head up, let him come up. Release your left hand from his head, and use that arm either to hit a headlock (page 91) or come under his far arm and hit a pancake (pp. 92–93). As you headlock or pancake him, use your overhook (right) arm to pull him forward and therefore off of his support.

★ Cobra or Spladdle

If your opponent lifts up his right knee, reach under it with your right arm and pull his knee tight into your chest so that his head is trapped (a). At the same time, use your right leg to hook his left leg. Once in this position, sit on your hip (b). If you haven't hooked the opponent's right leg securely, do so when you are down on your hip, then roll him to his back (c). This can also be done when he is on his feet.

a

b

c

Leg Block

If you are unable to sprawl and your opponent is in deeply on the single leg, grab his left lat (the side of his chest) with your right arm, and his right arm with your left arm. Then, step your right leg forward to block his right thigh, as shown. Pull up on his lat, pull his right arm forward and underneath you, and lift his thigh with your leg as you drive into him.

Kick-Over

If your opponent comes up between your legs, grab his right ankle with your left hand (a), then kick your leg over (b). This move is best done just as he comes underneath you.

a

b

Blocking His Head

See chapter 5, Freestyle Turns, pages 181–182.

COUNTERS DOWN ON THE MAT WITH HIS HEAD TO THE OUTSIDE

Cross Face Spin-Around

Cross face your opponent, turning his head to the outside, and grab his left arm above the elbow, as shown. Circle back toward his right foot, keeping pressure on his head and shoulder. If you break his grip, simply continue to spin around behind him for the takedown. If you can't break his grip, you can scoop his right foot with your left foot, or you can put your head into his side and reach for his right foot or ankle. As you drive your head into him and pull his foot toward you, this should turn him away from you and allow you to get around behind him.

Cradle

If you are spinning around your opponent and he brings his right knee up, you can cradle him.

Leg Scissors

If you are able to get your opponent sprawled flat, use your left heel to hook his right arm (a). Then, step your left leg over his head (b), bringing him to his back, where you can put in a reverse half nelson.

a

b

COUNTERS TO LOW SINGLE LEG

Moves to counter an opponent who is shooting or who is in front of you include *Kneeling on His Back*, *Rolling Him Over His Head*, and the *Cobra.*

Kneel on His Back

If he has just shot in and is in front of you, you can simply squat forward, driving your knee into his back.

Rolling Him Over His Head

Turn your body and your right leg so that you are directly over your opponent. Then sit on his head and lock your arms around his waist (a). Sit back on your right hip (b) and roll him over to his back.

a

b

Cobra

Similar to the Cobra described as a counter to a high single (page 40), as your opponent shoots a low single you can reach for his right knee. Lock around it (a), block his head with your right knee (b), and lift him over to his back. Unlike the situation when your opponent has a high single, you probably won't be able to hook his left ankle with your right leg since he is holding it.

a

b

COUNTERS TO A LOW SINGLE LEG WHEN HE IS BEHIND YOU

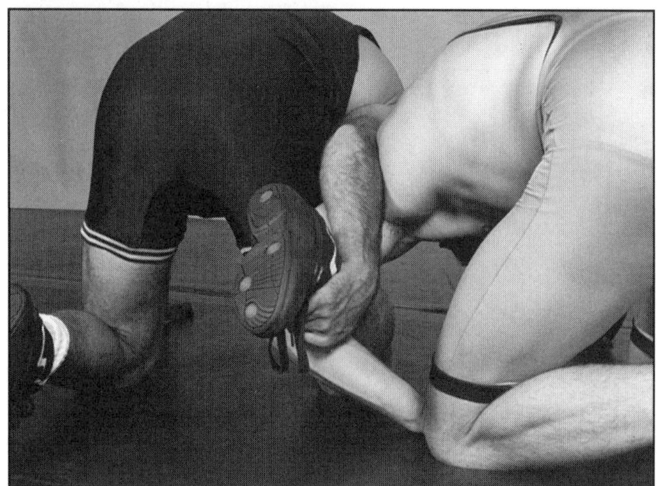
a

b

★Wizzer

If you were able to get the wizzer in as your opponent shot the low single, but he was still able to spin to the side of you, use your wizzer arm to grab your own ankle (a). Have your left leg out as a post, and sit on his left arm. This makes it very difficult for him to either come up to his feet or to reach above your knee.

Counter to the Wizzer

Place your left hand on your own thigh (b) and use this to lever into your opponent as you step behind him (c).

c

Kick-Out

Use your right hand to hold your opponent's head down so that he cannot come up (a). Put your left foot close enough so you have power to push with it, but far enough away so that he can't reach it. Straighten your ankle and point the toes of your right foot straight back so that your foot will come out easier. Push back into him first, and then pull your right leg out hard.

a

At the same time, reach your left arm back to his right hip so that you can turn in a tight circle (b). Once your foot is free, pivot on your left foot and spin behind him.

b

Stepping Over His Back

Make sure you have your opponent's head planted on the mat (as just described under *Kick-Out*), then step your left leg over his back (a). Then, either lock your hands around his left thigh or use your left arm to reach around his waist (b). Use your right leg to block his head and shoulders, and lift him over to his back (c).

a

b

c

HIGH CROTCH/HEAD-TO-THE-OUTSIDE SINGLE

Traditionally it has been taught that you should always shoot a single leg with your head to the inside to avoid a cross face, but if your hips are underneath you, this is not a major problem. In fact, if you do not take your opponent down with the initial "high crotch" (a), it is actually better to change your inside arm so that it is around his knee and your hand is on his calf—essentially a single leg with your head to the outside (b).

a

b

Penetration Step

You can lead with either the inside or outside leg. The "classic" high crotch involves leading with the outside (right) leg and going down on your inside knee. Whether you have control of your opponent's arm, elbow, or wrist, throw it back over you. Duck your head just enough to get it underneath his left arm, then snap your head back to help throw his arm and body past you. You should turn your chest away from him since this directs your right shoulder (and him) behind you. At the same time, your left arm should be reaching high in his crotch so that you end up with the left side of your chest and your left hip tight into him. If he's leaning into you or you throw his arm back hard enough, he will often go directly to the mat (a).

a

You can also lead with your inside leg (b), which probably gives you better penetration. If you need to, continue to drive into him by going down on your inside knee. Rather than throwing your left arm high into the crotch, it is acceptable (and in some cases better) to place that arm initially behind the knee. This is because your opponent is less powerful at his knee than in his hips, and if you do not finish the move with the initial shot, you have a much better chance of controlling him if you are at his knee than at his hip.

b

TIE-UPS AND SET-UPS

Elbow Control

The opponent's left hand is on your right arm or shoulder and you are grabbing his left arm just above the elbow, as shown. Your left arm can be either free or controlling his right shoulder or wrist. You need to be able to lift his left arm up enough to get your head underneath it. He can sometimes stop you from clearing his arm if he is controlling your right shoulder (with his thumb and fingers "pinching" your shoulder). If you find you cannot clear his arm because of this, you will need to use your left arm to come across and knock his arm off your shoulder, before or as you are initiating the move.

Inside Control

The only problem with throwing a high crotch from inside control (a) is that after you throw the opponent's arm back, you might have problems bringing your right arm forward without him underhooking it (b). To avoid this, you should "reach for your gun": After you have snapped his arm back, keep circling your arm behind you and then bring it forward fast and tight to your thigh (c), just as if you were reaching for a gun in a holster.

a

b

c

Controlling the Wrist (or He's Controlling Yours)

Just as with Inside Control, you must "reach for your gun" to clear your arm.

Single-Leg Set-ups

If you're doing a head-to-the-outside single rather than high crotch, you need to only clear your opponent's left arm rather than throw it behind you. You can use any of the set-ups for the single leg to do this.

Underhook

See the Underhook-Offense section on page 57.

FINISHES AS A CONTINUATION OF THE PENETRATION STEP

Throw Him Behind You

As just described, you can take your opponent directly to the mat simply by throwing him behind you. The keys are to have him pushing into you, throwing him hard with your right arm, arching your back, and throwing your head back to help drive his arm—and therefore him—behind you.

Change to a Double

The opponent's hips should be square to you for you to do this. If he has too much of an angle, you will not be able to get your left arm out.

Right after you hit on your left knee, pick it up and step across him as you drive off of your right foot, as shown. Let go of his left arm and use your right arm to control the outside of his left thigh. Throw your left arm across to control his right thigh. As you bring your arm across, you need to keep it in tight to his hips to prevent him from catching that arm. It is an explosive move—you are on your knee for only an instant; you hit on it and then immediately bring it up and step across. Once you are up on your feet and controlling both thighs, you can use any of the double-leg finishes.

Single-Leg Finish

If your opponent is no longer directly in front of you but has "turned the corner" (turned his right hip into you), it may not be possible to change to a double. Instead, change to a single by pushing off your right foot and driving into him with your head and shoulder just as for the double-leg finish. Rather than change your left arm to come across to his right thigh, just keep control of his left knee and come up with the single leg, as shown. Once up on your feet, you can do one of the finishes for when your head is to the outside (page 53), or adjust your head to either be in his ribs or on his thigh, whichever you feel more comfortable with.

FINISHES IF YOU GET STUCK ON THE MAT WITH BOTH KNEES DOWN

If you shoot a high crotch and get stopped underneath your opponent, change your arm control so that your left arm is around his knee and your right arm is over his calf (a). He will usually counter you by putting most of his weight down on his left leg and holding your inside arm so that you can't reach across and change to a double (b). If he isn't sprawled back too much and your hips are fairly tight to him, you can:

a

b

Drive Through Him

Drop your right hand to the back of the opponent's heel as you drive your shoulder into his thigh to take him backward.

Drop and Spin Behind Him

If your opponent is blocking your left arm so that you can't bring it across to change to a double, drop your head behind his thigh, grab the inside of his ankle, and then drive into him with your head and shoulder, picking up his foot as you do so, as shown.

Grab Both Heels

If your hips are in deep, drop your right hand down to grab the back of your opponent's left heel, reach your left arm behind his right heel, as shown, and drive into him.

Lift and Turn

Lock your hands around your opponent's thigh and hold his thigh tight to your chest. Raise your chest up, which, if you are tight enough, raises his left leg so that it comes off the mat. From this position, pivot on your left knee and drive into him.

Swing His Legs in Front of You

If you have your opponent's leg off the mat (as just described under *Lift and Turn*), use your left arm to reach behind and around his right leg. Pull his right leg down and in front of you and then grab it with your right arm (a). This causes him to slide off your left shoulder. Finish by planting your left arm on the mat on the far side of his hips (b).

a

b

Double When He Is Blocking Your Arm

Pick your right foot up and position it so that you can push off it to drive straight across the opponent and over your left knee, as shown below. This shifts his weight to his right leg and makes it hard for him to keep blocking your left arm. When you feel as if you're going to fall over your left knee, step your left leg across to the outside of his left leg so you are blocking it. As you are stepping, change to a double leg.

Sit-Back

If your opponent reaches around your waist with either arm, grab it with your right arm, as shown. Then, lift him as high as you can, arch your back, and take him over to his back.

Dump

Your opponent's weight needs to be off his left foot. Drive your shoulder into his left thigh as you pull his left leg underneath you and set him on his butt, as shown. Finish by circling toward his legs.

Fake Dump to a Double

If his legs are far apart making it difficult to change to a double, fake a dump; this brings his legs closer together, enabling you to grab both legs and drive him the other way.

FINISHES WHEN HE IS SPRAWLING BACK

Lift His Leg

As the opponent tries to sprawl back, if you keep your left arm tight around his knee and grab his calf with your hand, his leg will come off the mat (a). Then pivot on your left knee and spin around behind him to finish. If you are controlling him with your outside (right) arm and he sprawls back, his leg will come free rather than lift up (b).

a

b

Turn His Foot Out

If you can still reach your opponent's left foot, use your right hand to grab the bottom of his foot and control his heel. (If he's sprawled back, he will be on his toes, and his heels will be up.) Turn and lift his foot, as shown. This should turn his body away from you so that you can come up behind him.

Sag and Then Lift

If you can't pick up your opponent's leg because he is in a very stable position, keep holding his leg at his knee but sag your hips backward onto your heels; this will raise his heel. This movement takes the weight off his foot so that you can grab the back of his heel and lift him as just described, or grab the inside of his ankle and drive into him.

FINISHES WITH YOUR HEAD TO THE OUTSIDE, ON YOUR FEET

Dump

This is very similar to the dump with the head to the inside (pp. 15–16). Have downward pressure on your opponent's left thigh with your left shoulder (see photo below), and step your right foot back, circling him down to the mat.

Dump Variant

Alternatively, by shifting your right hand to your opponent's right calf and lifting up on it as you drive down on his thigh, you can dump him without circling.

FINISHES WHEN YOU ARE DOWN ON THE MAT AND HE IS AROUND YOUR WAIST

This is not a position you typically try to reach, but one you may get into when the opponent counters you (e.g., see *Scoot Behind Him*, page 56).

Split His Legs

First step your left and then your right leg over the opponent's left leg so that you have his legs split. Use your right knee to help lift his right leg, then drive into him taking him to his back, as shown.

Stepping Over Him With Your Hips Up

Step your right leg over your left leg and both of your opponent's legs, turning your back to his chest as you go (a). Then scissors your right leg under and your left leg over (b) and put in a half nelson or reverse nelson.

a

b

Stack Him

If you can hook the opponent's left elbow, you can try to drive straight into him, taking him toward his back (a). If you can't drive him back enough to get the takedown or back points, keep holding his left leg while stepping your left leg over your right leg up toward his head (b). If you can keep his arm and leg tight, you can stack him on his shoulders (c).

b

c

Drive Him to His Back

Even if you don't have your opponent's elbow hooked, you may be able to drive your left shoulder into his gut to get him toward his back, as shown. Unless your left arm is out, you still won't have control for a takedown, but from this position you can reach for his head to put in a half nelson.

Change to a Double

If you try to hook your opponent's left arm to stack him and he pulls his arm out, you may simply be able to sag your hips back, pop your head out, change to a double, and get control for the takedown.

COUNTERS TO HIGH CROTCH/HEAD-TO-THE-OUTSIDE SINGLE

Drive His Shoulder to the Side

Either hip into the opponent or use your left hand to push his right shoulder out (so that it is not on your thigh). At the same time squat to lower your chest, and then drive directly over him, as shown.

Back Roll

If your opponent comes up off his knees (a), squat underneath him and use your left arm to reach between his thighs. Post your right hand in back of you, or if possible, on his head, and then lift him directly over to his back (b). If possible, pinch his right arm with your legs as you finish so that you can hold him on his back.

a

b

Scoot Behind Him

One of the most common counters to the head on the outside single is to try to scoot behind the opponent. This is a scramble position that usually starts when the defensive man has started to sprawl, and the man in on the single chops the knee so that his opponent goes down to his hip (a and b). The wrestler on his butt needs to scoot his hips out to get the offensive man's shoulder off his thigh.

a

b

If he is able to reach in the crotch, he should be able to scoot around and hook in his legs to finish (c). Or, in freestyle, he could roll him through to get tilt points.

Counter to the Roll

A counter to this roll is to step across your opponent as he is throwing you. To do this, you need to let go of his right knee, post on your head, and throw your hips across him (d and e).

c

d

e

UNDERHOOK OFFENSE

The Underhook

An underhook is a tie-up in which your arm is under your opponent's arm and your hand is on his shoulder or upper back, as shown. Whenever you have an underhook, your opponent has an overhook (and different offensive possibilities of his own). It is therefore essential that you are lifting his arm and elbow with your underhook, thus controlling him. If he does control your arm, he has an excellent opportunity to hit a fireman's carry, so your other arm should either be controlling his wrist or be in front of you so you can block with it.

It is easy to get an underhook on some opponents because they will wrestle with their arms and elbows out. But to underhook an opponent who keeps his elbows in, you must grab his head with your left arm and jerk it away from the side you want to underhook. This will bring his elbow out so that you can underhook him.

FINISHES TO THE UNDERHOOK

Shrug

If the opponent's arm is very limp, duck your head as you throw his left arm over you. At the same time, use your left hand to control his wrist or to reach across his waist, as shown.

Leg Snatch

If your opponent's arm is too tight to shrug completely by, throw it up as far as possible. This will clear his left leg, enabling you to reach down with your left arm and grab him at the knee (see photo). Then drop your right arm down to lock your hands around his knee. Make sure you're grabbing him at his knee, since that is the weakest part of his leg.

★Ankle Pick

Step your right hip in front of the opponent's left hip, and with your hip and leg, raise his left leg so that all his weight is on his right foot. Besides lifting him, you want to be driving him over his right foot, shifting all his weight over it. As you bring your foot down to the mat, put it just to the outside of his right ankle to block it. Also, be pulling his shoulder down with your underhook so that his head is below yours, as shown. By using your ankle as a block, you can usually drive him over it and not have to grab his ankle with your hand. However, to make sure he doesn't step over it, you should grab his right ankle with your left hand. All through the move, your weight is over his right ankle—you never lean back, but drive directly over his right ankle, using your underhook to drive his head over his knee and down to the mat.

Single or High Crotch

Just as you did for the ankle pick in the previous move, step your hip in as if you're trying to elevate the opponent's left leg. If you can elevate it and he leaves his right leg close, ankle pick him. He will usually try to square in front of you, though. When he does, his left leg is open for a single or high crotch. When you hit one of these, throw his left arm up and over you with your underhook.

Leg Snatch

You can also get into a single leg if your opponent is crunching in on your elbow with his overhook, making your underhook ineffective. You need to step behind him, hooking his left ankle with your heel, as shown. Then drive into him, shifting his weight to his right foot, thus making it easy to snatch his left leg up with your left arm.

Double Leg

Start by hipping into your opponent or jerking the underhook to get him to face you. As he is facing you, not after he has already faced you and is in a good defensive position, step into the double, leading with either your inside or outside leg, and with your head on the right side (opposite your underhook).

Drag

With the underhook, pull your opponent straight down toward your right foot. As you pull him below your shoulders, bring your left arm across, palm up, chopping down on his left arm (a), thus clearing it. Step your left foot back so he doesn't fall into it. The underhook arm pulls him down and your left arm clears his arm and finishes the move. As you bring your left arm down over his, pull out your underhook so it doesn't get caught (b).

a

b

Knee Pick

Circle away from the opponent's right leg so he will step it toward you. Just as he steps, block the outside of his knee with your left hand and drive him over it. Change your underhook so you are controlling around his back, and use it to help drive him over his knee. The opponent won't always go down with one step as in an ankle pick, but keep driving him over his knee, and eventually he will go down. If possible, as you step across to block his knee, step on his right foot, as shown, making it impossible for him to shift his weight.

Duckunder

If you have your opponent's wrist or he has yours, circle toward the underhook so he has to step into you with his right foot. As he steps, hit a duckunder and finish as described in the upcoming *Duckunders* section (page 75).

OVER-UNDERHOOK

Basic Over-Underhook

This position involves an overhook on one side and an underhook on the other side. Your head and most of your weight should be on your overhook side (the opponent's underhook side). By being "heavy" on his power arm, you eliminate a lot of his offense. It is important to remember that any time you have an over-underhook, your opponent has the same tie-up, and therefore he can do the same moves as you. Included in this section is the bodylock position (page 63), which is essentially an over-underhook with your hands locked around his lower back.

FINISHES WITH THE OVER-UNDERHOOK

★Hip Toss

This is a throw, or toss, in which most of the power comes from your legs and hips. As in most throws, the key is getting both of your hips through. It is best to get your opponent circling toward your underhook side, and then to do your backstep in the opposite direction. This helps you get your hips all the way through. You can also set him up by easing your weight up from his right arm and standing up a little straighter, making him think that he can bear hug you. As he steps in to bear hug, his forward movement will help you get your hips through as you backstep in the opposite direction. When you backstep (page 4), have your knees bent so your hips are lower than his. Once both your hips are through (a), straighten your knees so his feet will come off the mat. Pull down on your overhook side and lift up with your underhook to finish the throw (b).

a

b

Hip Toss With an Underhook and Wrist Control

This move can also be done if you have no overhook, but just your opponent's wrist.

Sag Throw

Step your left leg to the outside of your opponent's right leg so that you are blocking his thigh (a). As you step, your hips should be lower than his (otherwise he can hip toss you). It is best if you can lock your hands, but if you can't, the throw can be done with the over-underhook. From this position, just fall down on your right shoulder (b), and then turn on top of him.

a

b

Hip Toss to the Underhook Side

The opponent can prevent you from doing a sag throw by keeping his hips and his right leg back so you cannot block them. He opens himself, though, for you to step in with your overhook side (left) hip. Lock your hands, pull his chest tight into yours, and pull him down in front of you.

Lace Leg

As with the sag throw, this move can be done with your hands either locked or unlocked. Lace your left leg around your opponent's right thigh and leg, and step your right foot close to him so that your hips are tight with his. From here arch back, twisting toward your overhook (left) side and lifting his leg (a). Even after you hit on your shoulder (b), your foot should still be hooked and lifting his leg until you finish on top of him.

Counter to the Lace Leg

After your opponent has laced his leg and steps his right foot up to begin the throw, lower your hips and step your right leg up to trap his right leg (c). Then drive into him and take him down to the mat.

a

b

c

★Leg Trip

Circle toward your overhook side so the opponent is stepping his left leg toward you. As he steps his leg, step with your right leg so that it is to the outside of his leg and your knee is blocking his knee. As you step, reach with your overhook (left) arm across and into his crotch (a). Then, pull down with your right arm, lift with your left arm, and pull him over your knee (b). Take him sideways over your knee, not backward.

a

b

★Inside Trip

From a bodylock position (your arms need to be around the lower half of your opponent's back), circle away from the side you have the arm trapped on (his right side) toward his left side. As you step with your right foot, and shift all of your weight on that foot, pull him toward you, getting him to step his right leg forward. Your left foot initially steps back, as if you were going to continue to circle him, but don't touch your left foot to the mat. You need to keep your weight forward into him, and then as he steps with his right foot, swing your left leg into him, lacing around his right leg from the inside (a). Then continue to drive into him (b). If you do not have your weight forward when you circle away from your opponent, you will need to put your left foot down on the mat for balance, and then shift your weight before you can pick up your left foot to step back into him. That would usually delay you enough to make the move ineffective.

This move can also be done from an over-underhook, but it is more difficult since you don't have as much control. You can do it to either side, but as just described, you want to be circling away from the leg that you are going to trip. Therefore, if you are going to trip the opponent's left leg and have an underhook on that side, circle toward his right. Shift your weight as just described, then step behind his left leg and trip him backward.

a

b

Underarm Spin

This move works best if your opponent is pushing into you with his chest, but has his hips back. With your left foot, step past his left foot and throw your left arm under his left arm (a). You should be deep enough so that your left shoulder is underneath his arm. As you step and throw your arm, arch straight back toward his left knee, holding his arm tight to your chest. On your way back, turn away from his body and land on one or both knees, still controlling his arm (b). You should be blocking both of his legs with your body and be tight to them. Don't go flat—you won't be able to block him. As you hit, continue to roll through, pulling him over you (c). When you finish, get into the habit of pulling your inside (left) arm out and reaching across his body (d). It is quite common to end up to his side rather than directly in front of him (e).

a

b

c

d

e

Pop Your Head Out Finish

Pop your head out and go behind the opponent.

Roll Underneath Finish

Keep his arm tight, turn your head and left shoulder down and back toward his feet, roll to your left hip (f) and pull him over. If you have his arm tight, you can get a tremendous amount of pressure on his shoulder.

Roll Over Him finish

Keep pressure on your opponent's left arm with your chest and right arm, and reach over his head with your left arm to grab his chin (g). Walk around to his front, then turn your left hip down. Keep his arm and chin tight as you take him to his back (h).

g

h

i

Counter to the Underarm Spin

Just as you feel your opponent starting to spin through, shift your hips and your weight backward (i). This creates a lot of space between you and his body, and he will just fall down on the mat in front of you, either flat on his back or on his side, and have no leverage to pull you over him (j).

j

Knee Block

Circle toward your underhook side so your opponent is stepping his right leg toward you. Just as he steps, reach your underhook arm across to the outside of his right knee. Turn your hand thumb down so your palm is against his knee (a). Continue to circle away as you block his knee. As he starts to go down, pull your right arm out and reach around his waist. Don't go down to the mat until he is down. This move can also be done by using your overhook (left) arm to block his right knee (b).

a

b

★Counter to the Knee Block

As the opponent starts to block your knee as just described, use your overhook (left) arm to trap his right arm and hit a lateral drop (c). This is why it was emphasized in the knee block to pull your right arm out as soon as your opponent starts to go down so that he can't lateral drop you.

c

Single Leg

You will be grabbing your opponent's right leg (the side that he has an underhook on you). You cannot simply reach down and grab that leg because his underhook will prevent it. Instead, step toward his right leg and drop all of your weight straight down, pulling your underhook out as you go, and then lock around his knee.

Left Knee Block

If you attempt to drop down to the opponent's right leg for a single and he steps that leg back, grab his left knee with your right hand. Keep your left elbow to your side to keep his right arm blocked and drive across him.

Slide Behind Him

Reach back with your left hand to grab the opponent's right wrist. Pull his wrist off your back so that his right arm is next to his side (a). Drop your hips to his right side, blocking his right arm with your chest, then continue to spin around him (b).

a

b

Near-Arm Far-Leg

This move is similar to the near-arm far-leg described later (page 81), except that your underhook control will take the place of the near arm. First circle toward your underhook to get your opponent stepping toward you with his right foot. Drop down to your knees and reach around his right knee, placing your left hand around his calf (a). At the same time, use your right underhook arm to pull his left shoulder down. Then lift his right leg up and continue to pull his left shoulder down, circling him toward you to take him to the mat (b).

a

b

Bear Hug

Lower your hips and step in between your opponent's legs with your right leg to penetrate. Lock your hands down around his waist, including his arm if you can. Finish with any of the finishes described in the upcoming *Bear Hugs* section (pp. 86–87).

Crunch

If your opponent steps his left leg back (either because you are circling toward it or you are attempting to grab it), step your right hip in and slide your overhook arm up into a headlock position (a). Your left forearm will be across his right collarbone. Pull his chest tight into you (b). From this position, you can get a tremendous amount of pressure and just "crunch" him to his back.

a

b

Shrug

As described in the underhook section (page 58), you can use your underhook arm to throw the opponent's arm over you. It is usually more difficult from this position, though, since he usually has more weight on your underhook arm. Because of this, a good time to hit the shrug is as you are pummeling and just after you have gotten underhook control on that side.

Lateral Drop

The best time to hit a lateral drop is when you opponent is pushing into you. You can set this up by first pushing into him or by reaching for his right leg, making him step that leg back and lean into you with his chest. Step your right foot to the outside of his left foot (a), and then circle your left foot backward as you pull down on his right arm (b). Do not take him directly over his right foot, instead pull or circle him toward the front, where he has no support.

a

b

Counter to a Lateral Drop

Step your right leg to the outside of your opponent's left leg and come in between his legs with your left arm (c).

c

BASIC SEAT BELT

To apply the seat belt, place your arm around your opponent's lower back controlling his far hip. Although your arm is behind him rather than in front, it is controlling him just as a seat belt would, hence the name. Your opponent's only initial option is to apply a wizzer, since that is all he can do to keep you from getting behind him.

From a Single Leg

If you're in on a high single leg either down on the mat (page 15) or up on your feet (page 14), and the opponent is countering with a wizzer, you can slide your arm up from his leg to around his waist. This will put you in the seat belt position. (The decision to use the single leg or the seat belt depends on how good you are at each position and how tight your single leg and his wizzer are.)

From an Underhook

Another way to get into the seat belt on your feet is from an underhook on the opponent's left side. Circle to that side (page 59) and simply drop your arm from under his shoulder to around his back.

He Counters With a Wizzer

If you are in control of your opponent either down on the mat or on your feet with your arm around his back, and he counters with a wizzer, he will be putting you in the seat belt position.

FINISHES WITH THE SEAT BELT FROM YOUR FEET

Single Leg

Step behind the opponent and hook his left ankle with your right heel. Drive into him, making him shift his weight to his right foot, then grab his left knee. The situation for this move usually arises if he is wizzering hard enough that you do not have good control with the seat belt—you will not be able to get your right arm down to lock up with your other hand unless you drive into him to get his weight shifted.

Hip Toss

This move works best if you can grab the opponent's wrist as you throw him, but it works even if you can't grab the wrist. Simply do a back step to his right foot, making sure you get your hips all the way through. Finish the move as described earlier (pp. 60–61).

Throw

Put your left hand on your opponent's right chest or shoulder. Step your left foot over to his right foot so that your hips are in tight to him. From here, do a back arch, exploding your hips in, pushing on his shoulder, and pulling back on his hip. This move can also be done with an overhook if you grab your left forearm with your overhook arm.

FINISHES WITH THE SEAT BELT FROM DOWN ON THE MAT

Reaching Over His Head

To have power down on he mat with the seat belt, your right shoulder should be nearly on top of your opponent's back (a). If there is a gap between your shoulder and his side, he will have much more power with his wizzer and will be able to put a lot of pressure down on your shoulder, making the seat belt ineffective. Reach over the top of his head and grab his chin with your left hand and turn it away (b). Then, pull your left elbow down to your side, which pulls his shoulder down (c). As you pull him down, pull him toward you so that you are taking him in a short circle rather than directly over his support arm. Keep control of his chin (with his head twisted) even after you get him on his back so that he can't bridge.

a

b

c

Pull Him Back

If you start to reach over your opponent's head to do the move just described and he comes up with you, you can just pull him back with the seat belt.

Bear Hug

If your opponent comes up with you and reaches for your left arm, before he has a chance to pull you underneath him, lock up a bear hug (with or without his arm trapped), and take him to his back.

Crunch

Even if your opponent is not reaching across for your arm, if you pull him tight enough into you with the seat belt, you can reach underneath and lock your hands around the base of his ribs. You can apply tremendous pressure and cause him to bail out (i.e., let go of the wizzer to go to his base, giving you control). The key is to lock your hands correctly. You want your right hand to be facing down and your left hand to be facing up. The bony part of your right hand will then be driving into his ribs, creating a lot of pressure.

Drive Across His Ankles

Sag your weight back toward the opponent's feet, making his wizzer less effective. Use your seat belt arm to grab his right ankle, then drive across him.

Limp Arm Out

This is a means of getting your arm free by dropping your shoulder to the mat, essentially letting your arm go limp. Step over the opponent's left leg while keeping pressure into him with your right hip to get his weight over to his right side to make his wizzer less effective. This allows you to release your right arm from around his back. Twist your arm inward so it is palm up, then "limp arm out" by driving your shoulder down toward the mat and pulling your arm forward. Before he has time to react, get behind him for control.

Pull His Inside Ankle Up

Sag back and walk around your opponent enough so that you can grab his left ankle with your left hand. You can spin further behind him to get control or drive him forward off his base, unless his wizzer is still tight. In that case, release your seat belt and use your right arm to grab his left thigh. Then drive your shoulder into his butt, making him release the wizzer.

Stepping Over His Back

Before stepping over your opponent's back, it is safest to first sag back toward his feet to take the power away from his wizzer. Then, step your right leg over his back and hook it in. If you are a tall and lanky wrestler, you may be able to step over your opponent's back without sagging back if you are long enough so that your left knee is still on the mat as a brace. Otherwise, your opponent can raise his butt up, grab your left arm, and use his wizzer arm to pull you underneath him.

COUNTERS TO THE SEAT BELT

On Your Feet

Face Him

Wizzer hard and drop your hips to take power away from your opponent's seat belt. Turn to face him but make sure your hips are back so he can't bear hug you.

Fireman's Carry

See the upcoming section on Fireman's Carry set-ups (pp. 81–82).

Down on the Mat

Wizzer

You eliminate your opponent's power if you can drive his shoulder down with the wizzer. You should try to keep your head and shoulder above his head and shoulder but at the same time don't raise up so much that he can pull you back (page 71).

Elevate His Leg

If your opponent steps over your right ankle, wizzer hard to get his shoulders down and grab his right arm with your left arm (a). Pull his arm underneath you and elevate his leg with your leg (b).

a

b

DUCKUNDERS

This series of moves involves ducking your head under one of your opponent's arms.

Penetration Step

To penetrate for a duckunder, step with your outside foot, hit on your inside knee, and then come up immediately. You want to duck your head just enough to get it under your opponent's arm, and then use your head and right arm to help snap his arm back.

Tieups/Set-ups for the Duckunder

In all of the set-ups, you want to get your head underneath your opponent's arm. This may require nothing more than good arm control and an explosive move. It helps to push down on the arm you are going to be ducking under so that he reacts by pushing it up and out. Or, you can pull down on his opposite side, which typically lifts up the side you want to duck under.

Head and Arm Control

Pull your opponent's head down with your left hand while you duck under his left arm. You may want to drive his left elbow in first so that he reacts by lifting his left arm up.

Lat and Arm Control

From an underhook, control your opponent's right lat, and pull down on it as you duck under the opposite side.

Inside Control on Both Sides

Drive your opponent's left elbow in, then when he reacts by pushing it out, throw it out and back over you as you duck under it (see page 48). Or, you can fake a duckunder to one side, then when he counters, duck under the other side.

Wrist Control

Whether you have a grip on your opponent's wrist or he has yours, you can either hit the move directly to one side or fake a duckunder one way, and when he counters he will open up on the other side.

If he has your wrist, it may be difficult to free it as you duck under him. The key to this is to turn your palm backward (which weakens his grip) and stretch his arm by blocking his underarm on your neck and shoulder. This essentially pulls his hand off your wrist (a).

a

Underhook or Seat Belt Control

If you grab your opponent's opposite wrist or he grabs yours, you can duck under that side.

Headlock Position

With your hands locked ready to do a headlock, fake a headlock toward your opponent's left side. When he reacts and shifts his weight, hit a duckunder (b). Be aware that when he is locked up for a headlock like this, he can also duck under you if you don't have him tight enough.

Head Control and He Reaches

When you get head control, your opponent will often reach up to tie up your head or shoulder. As he reaches (not after he has gained control of your head), you should drive his arm up by hitting it above the elbow, then duck under him.

b

Finishes to the Duckunder

Keep His Head

Keep control of your opponent's head or arm on the left side and bring him down to the mat.

Change to a Double in the Standing Position

After you are under your opponent's arm, change your right arm to control his upper left thigh and put your left arm around his waist and control his far hip (a). From here lift him up and either hook his right leg on the way down in a turk ride (pp. 10–11) or lift him and dump him in front of you.

Go Behind Him

After you have initially hit on your knee and are underneath your opponent's arm, bounce up and come completely behind him. Bring your left arm across and control his left thigh (b). You do not want to leave your left arm across his chest or belly since he could grab it, block your left ankle (c), and roll you. The difference between this position and that just described is that in the former position you have your opponent's legs straddled and your hips low and tight to the left leg, making it difficult for him to step his left leg in front to use it as a block (even if he did, he wouldn't have any power).

a

b

c

★Bear Hug

After you get your head under your opponent's arm, bring your left leg across to the outside of his right leg so you're blocking it. At the same time, bear hug him (d), trapping his right arm if possible. Once locked up, take him over the leg you have blocked or simply "crunch" him over backward.

Double Leg

Another option just after you get your head under your opponent's arm is to step your left knee across to block his right knee, change your arms to around his knees, and use your head to drive him over as you lift his legs (e).

d

e

FIREMAN'S CARRY

The fireman's carry is a takedown in which you attack the same-side arm and leg of your opponent. During part of the move, you end up with your opponent up on your shoulders, just as a fireman would be carrying a victim. There are various penetration steps for the fireman's carry. Since the finishes are continuations of the various penetration steps, the finishes will be discussed along with the penetration steps.

In this move, you can lead with your inside leg, your outside leg, or drop to both knees at the same time without leading with either leg. The key part of the fireman's carry is holding your opponent's right arm tight. Part of this control is your hand holding his arm against your shoulder. In addition, you should use your right forearm and elbow to pinch his forearm next to your side, as shown. Keep control of his arm even after you have taken him down to t he mat since this should help you finish with back points. One last general instruction is that as you take him to the mat you should release his left leg so that your left arm doesn't get caught between his legs.

Stepping With Your Inside Leg First

Driving Through Him

With all fireman's carries, your head is going to the outside of your opponent's left hip. You are typically going to be reaching with your left hand between his legs and grabbing his left leg, but the move can also be done by just blocking the outside of his hip or knee. Continue your penetration by driving into him, going down on your right knee. Straighten your back, which lifts his feet off the mat (a). Pull his arm down, throw his legs over your head, and pop your head out as you take him to his back (b).

a

Taking Him Sideways

A second option is to lead with your inside knee but turn perpendicular to your opponent and go down to both knees (c). The picture shows the left arm around his left leg, which is all right, but you can also reach up between his thighs to his butt, allowing you to lift his crotch as you pull down on his arm to take him to the mat. If hit explosively, you don't have to go down to your shoulder. It should also be pointed out that you not only want to hold his arm tight, but you also want to be pulling his shoulder down tight to yours. If you have him tight like this, it is easy to get his feet off the mat simply by straightening your back (d). However, if there is space between his shoulder and yours (e), it is hard to get his feet off the mat and difficult to complete the move.

b

c

d

e

Stepping With Your Outside Leg First

Sit-Through

When you lead with your outside leg (a), one option is to take a long step with your inside (left) leg between your opponent's legs (b), almost as if doing a sit-out. Go down to your right shoulder and throw his legs over (c). This is the worst of the finishes, though, since this gives your opponent his best chance of stepping over your left leg, scissoring your arm, and holding you on your back (d).

a

b

c

d

Driving Straight Through

In this finish, you don't hit and then turn, but keep your momentum going forward and drive straight through your opponent. Drop your outside knee right behind his foot (e) and then drive him over it (f and g). With each of the previous finishes your chest was facing away from him after you penetrated, but in this finish you turn 90 degrees into him. You can also drive straight through him without turning your chest (h), but you usually finish by shaking him off your head. This is a scramble position that is not as desirable as the other finishes.

e

f

g

h

Positional Finishes

These are finishes that can be done depending on how your opponent counters.

He Pulls His Arm Free

If he pulls his arm free, try either the Knee Pry or the High Crotch.

■ *Knee Pry.* If he has pulled free his arm and is straightening up before you have a chance to finish, lock both arms around his knee and pry down on that knee to set him on his butt. Do this just as he pulls his arm out and before he has a chance to sprawl back.

■ *High Crotch.* Change to the high crotch position by getting your hip in tight and stepping your right leg up. The various finishes from this position were previously described (pp. 46–53).

You Keep Control of His Arm but He Sprawls the Leg Back and You Lose It

From this position (a), you have several options:

■ *Block His Left Leg.* Bring your left arm across to the outside of his left knee. Block his knee with your palm, thumb down (b), pull his arm down, drive into him, and pry up on that knee.

■ *Block His Right Leg.* You can also block on the inside of his right leg and finish as in the previous move.

■ *Finish Around His Waist.* Bring your left arm up around his waist (c), pull down on his left arm, and throw him over you.

a

b

c

Your Head Gets Caught

If you finish the fireman's but you can't get your head out and he is scissoring your left arm so you can't free it (d), there are a few moves you can try:

■ *Drive Him to His Back.* Post on your head, get off your knees and up on your toes, and then circle either toward his feet or his head (e). Even if you still cannot get your head loose, you will put him to his back and likely cause him to bail out.

■ *Stack Him.* Either as a continuation of walking toward your opponent's head or as a single step with your left leg over your right leg and up toward his head (f), stack him (g).

■ *Step Over His Legs.* Drop your weight back to your left knee, and then step across his legs (h).

■ *Flip Over Him.* Flip straight across him (i) and turn toward his legs.

d

e

f

g

h

i

NEAR-ARM FAR-LEG

Basic Near-Arm Far-Leg

Unlike the fireman's carry, which involves attacking your opponent's same-side arm and leg, in this move you attack his right arm and left leg, or vice versa. As in the fireman's, the most important point is to keep his arm tight. Besides keeping it tight, you need to pull it down with you as you attack his leg. You can control his leg at the thigh or the knee (the knee is better), and you can put your head to the inside of his left thigh (a) or outside of his right thigh.

A third option is to put your head on the front of your opponent's right arm (on his biceps), and then pull his elbow toward you, essentially pinching his biceps (b). This keeps your head from getting caught, allows you to put pressure on his arm, and makes it difficult for him to sprawl and counter you with an underhook.

To finish the move, wherever your head is, go down to your left shoulder and throw his leg over (c). As with the fireman's carry, you should release his leg as you finish but keep his arm tight to take him to his back.

a

b

c

SET-UPS FOR THE FIREMAN'S CARRY OR NEAR-ARM FAR-LEG

In general, for either move it helps if you have your opponent stepping into you with the leg (left) that you are going to attack. In addition, you need to clear his free arm so that you can penetrate his legs without him blocking you.

Elbow or Arm Control

Have your head on your opponent's left shoulder, control his left arm with your right arm, and with your left arm push his right shoulder to clear it (page 47). Either circle toward his right leg and attack the left leg just as he steps forward with it, or drive into him and attack his left leg when he steps his right leg back.

Pull Down on His Head

One way of getting your opponent to move his head out of the way is to pull his head down so that he reacts by pulling it up. As you shoot in you need to clear his arm with your free arm.

Wizzer

If your opponent is in a seat belt position and on your side (page 69), it doesn't leave you with much offense. Use a hard wizzer to get him to face you (a); this should also force him to take a large step that spreads his feet fairly far apart, making it easy to come in between them for a fireman's carry. As you throw the move, you need to change your overhook arm to control his upper left arm.

Drag

If you have cleared your opponent's arm across his front (b), keep control of his arm and throw a fireman's to his left leg (c).

Two-On-One

As with the wizzer, you can get your opponent to square up to you by hitting into him with a two-on-one, as described later on page 103, under *Fireman's Carry*.

Fake One, Go for the Other

Controlling your opponent's arm and reaching for either move (fireman's carry or near-arm far-leg) is a good set-up for the other since he will usually step back the leg you are faking to and leave the other one open to attack.

Front Headlock

See the upcoming section, Front Headlocks, on page 100.

a

b

c

ARM DRAGS

The arm drag is designed to drag or move your opponent's arm. It can be used to set up another takedown or be a takedown in itself. With any of the different arm drags, one arm is a guide arm that starts to move his arm in the right direction; the other arm is the power arm, which hooks his arm and moves it the rest of the way.

Set-Ups for the Arm Drag

You Have His Wrist

The right arm (the one controlling the wrist) is the guide arm. The left hand may be free, be in a shallow underhook, or be controlling your opponent's head. Use your right hand to bring his left arm across his front and at the same time come across with your left arm and hook his left arm just above the elbow. You do not need to grab his arm, only hook it (a, next page). Once you have hooked his arm with your left arm (your power arm), you can release your right hand and it can be used for whatever finish you want.

He Has Your Wrist

Everything is the same as when you have your opponent's wrist except that to clear your wrist you have to slap it explosively to your left hip so that he loses his grip. If you do not move that guide arm across explosively, you will not break his grip and you will not be able to finish the move.

a

Inside Control

If you have inside control on both sides or have it on one side and the other arm is free (page 48, *a*), release his left arm with your right hand and rotate your arm and forearm to the outside of his forearm. Once your forearm is to the outside of his arm, bring it down and back across so that you start to drive his arm to the inside. Your guide (right) arm therefore goes in a complete circle: up, out, down, and then back in. At the same time, your left arm comes across and hooks his left arm above the elbow (b), clearing his side (c). The same drag works as he is reaching for your head or shoulder or when he already has control of either of them.

Redrag

When your opponent starts to drag you and hooks your left arm with his left arm (d), hook his arm and drag him (e).

Drag From an Underhook

This set-up is described earlier in the Underhook Offense section (page 59).

b

c

d

e

Finishes to the Arm Drags

Taking Him Directly to the Mat

As you drag your opponent (a), instead of using your power (left) arm to clear his arm across his chest, use it to pull his left arm and his shoulder down to the mat. At the same time hook your left leg under his left leg and scissors your right leg over it (b). The problem with this finish is that he has the potential to step over your legs and get not only the takedown but also back points.

Single or Double

Use the arm drag to clear your opponent's left side and make it easy to penetrate for a single leg or double leg (c).

Tripping Him Backward

Penetrate straight into your opponent and hook his left leg with your left leg (d). Have your forearm across his chest with his left arm blocked. Drive straight into him, taking him directly backward. As you hit, put both hands out to the side so that he cannot roll you as you hit.

a

b

c

d

ANKLE AND KNEE PICKS

In both pick takedowns, either your opponent's ankle or knee is being grabbed, or "picked." It is sometimes possible to pick up the ankle or knee, but the key point of the move is to block his leg and then drive him over it. If the leg that you are picking is firmly planted, he would be able to push off of it to counter you. Therefore, another key is to time the move as his weight is being shifted to the knee or ankle you are going to block, but before his foot is firmly planted and he has all his weight on it.

Controlling His Head

Circle toward your opponent's left side so that he is stepping toward you with his right foot. Just before he plants the right foot (his weight is not on it yet but he has nearly completed his step), stop circling and drive his head toward his right foot. Grab the outside of his ankle and drive over it (a).

a

If He Steps His Foot Back

If he steps his right foot back as you reach for it, drive back toward his left ankle and pick it.

INCORRECT ANKLE PICK

For all ankle picks, it is important to keep your head above your opponent's. If your head is below his, he could reach over your right arm and grab your head with his left arm, turn his head away, and grab your right arm with his right arm to shuck you.

b

From Down on the Mat

If you have stopped one of your opponent's takedown attempts down on the mat and then he steps his foot up close enough for you to grab (b), drive his head and his weight over it (c). Even if he doesn't step his foot up far enough to grab but you can reach his knee, block his knee and drive him over that.

c

Knee Pick From the Feet

From a head and arm tie-up, push into your opponent to make him step his left leg back. Then, as he starts to bring that leg back (while it is in the air), drive across him blocking the outside of his left knee (d) and drive him over it (e). He may not go down with a single step, but you are in position to run him over it.

d

e

From an Underhook

See the Underhook Offense section on page 58.

BEAR HUGS

Basic Bear Hug

The bear hug involves locking your arms around your opponent's back. To be effective, you need to get your hips tight to his, which means stepping in between his legs (see photo). It is better if you can trap an arm, and best if the arm you trap is on the same side your head is. You can get into the bear hug from various positions:

Bear Hug From a Single Leg

The various finishes described in the single-leg section are higher percentage finishes, but if you are having problems taking down your opponent with any of those finishes or if you are behind and need back points, a bear hug is a good finish. Pull him into you with the single leg so that he is hopping toward you. Just as he hops, release the single leg, drive into him, and lock around his waist.

Bear Hug While Pummeling

Pummeling is the repetitive motion of both wrestlers changing from an over-underhook on one side to the other side. As you are pummeling, if you can get an underhook on both sides, simply lock up the bear hug without an arm trapped. If you can't, just as you change your hands (you are changing from outside to inside control on the right and vice versa on the left), step your right leg between your opponent's legs, drop your hips lower than his, and trap his right arm as you lock up the bear hug low around his back.

Bear Hug From Behind Him

This is especially good to try if you plan on letting your opponent go anyway. If he has stood up and you are behind him with control around his waist, allow him to get his hip loose. This baits him to wizzer you. As he starts to do so, he has to turn into you, and as he does, step in and lock up your bear hug.

Bear Hug Finishes

Block His Opposite Knee

If you step up to block your opponent's left leg and he steps it back, step across with your left leg to block his right knee, and take him down (see *Sag Throw*, photos *a* and *b*, page 61).

Double Knee Block

After you have stepped your right leg up to block your opponent's left knee (page 61), use it to push his knee in and at the same time squeeze your left knee between your right knee and his left leg so that both of your legs are to the outside of his (a). Then just take him backward.

Hip Toss

Lower your hips below your opponent's and step your left hip in. You need to keep his chest tight to your chest so that as you rotate your hip and turn, you will pull him in front of you (b).

a

b

Greco-Roman Throw

The following finish can be used in any style of wrestling but is seen most frequently in Greco-Roman wrestling. As you step in to lock up the bear hug, rather than staying in front of your opponent, step your right leg behind his left leg. Turn perpendicular to him with your hips below his and pull his hips tight into you (c). Don't stop here, but in a continuous motion rotate counterclockwise and complete a full circle as you take him over to his back (d). Rather than taking him back at a 45-degree angle as described before (page 61), arch your hips under him and take him over in front of you.

Crunch Him

This is easiest to do when you are under both of his arms. Your hands should be locked around his lower back. Use your arms to pull his back in while using your shoulder or head to drive into his chest. Bend him straight back to complete the move.

Block His Knee/Sag Throw

See the *Sag Throw* in the Over-Underhook section on page 61.

Inside Trip

See *Inside Trip*, photos *a* and *b*, page 63.

c

d

COUNTERS TO THE BEAR HUG

Sag Your Hips

To sag describes the action of letting your entire body weight hang or sag on your opponent. The finishes to the bear hug just described all involve your opponent getting his hips tight to yours. If you can keep your hips sagged and have at least one of your arms blocking his hips (see photo), you could stop his offense.

Counter to the Sag

If your opponent is backing away from you and keeping his hips back, walk backward pulling him with you; this will bring his hips in. Make sure he does not trip you as you are backing up. If he has his hips sagged back, you have to be very cautious of trying to step into him to get your hips tighter because he could headlock you.

Push His Chin Away

Another way to counter the bear hug is to put both your hands under your opponent's chin and drive it up, sagging your hips back and down at the same time.

Headlock

If you can sag your hips enough so that you can get them through (especially if he is driving into you), your opponent is set up for a headlock (a).

Fake Headlock, Block Opposite Leg

If you attempt a headlock, your opponent will usually counter by shifting his weight to his left side. As he does, do these three things at the same time: Grab the right side of his neck and pull his head to your right; step your right leg to the outside of his left leg, therefore blocking it; and reach your left arm between his legs (b). From here, lift and pull him over your knee.

a

b

★ Front Sal To

When your opponent is straight in front of you and under both arms, overhook both of his arms, put your fists in his chest, bring your elbows in to break his grip, and step in and hit a back arch.

Lace Leg

This is a last resort move when your opponent has your hips tight and is starting to bend you back. Lace his leg on the same side you have an overhook, then complete the throw from the over-underhook (page 62).

SHORT OFFENSE

The moves described in the short offense section are—with one exception—moves done when both wrestlers are facing each other down on their knees. Since they are on their knees, they are "short," and hence the name short offense. The moves are divided into those done when the offensive wrestler has an arm and collar tie-up, an underhook, or a double overhook.

★ Head-Snap Run-Around

This is the one exception of the short offense section where both wrestlers do not start on their knees facing each other. However, after the initial step, both wrestlers are in the short offense position.

Head-Snap Run-Around When You Both Are on Your Feet

The key to an effective head-snap is hitting it as your opponent is stepping a foot forward (but before it is planted), thus shifting his weight forward. The simplest way to set up this situation is to start with a head and arm tie-up and push into him to make him step his right leg back (a). As he reacts and steps back into you, hit the "snap" just before his right foot comes down on the mat.

Another set-up is to fake a single-leg shot to make him step one leg back, which typically leaves his weight forward on the other leg. When you "snap" him, you essentially throw him down to the mat (b). Then, spin around behind your opponent. As you spin around him, the key step is blocking his right arm. As you start the spin, your left hand is initially blocking his arm (b), but then as you get farther around him, your right forearm comes over his head and blocks his right arm (c). If possible, post your right hand and arm on the mat to both block his right arm and to give you a brace to spin on as you go behind him. If you don't block his arm, even if you have spun three quarters of the way around him, it is easy for him to lower his shoulder, throw his arm back, and catch one or both of your legs, stopping the move (d).

a

b

c

d

After you have spun around behind him, do not reach deep around his waist with your left arm since he could easily use your momentum and roll you (e). Instead, control his left hip or thigh.

Head-Snap Run-Around as Your Opponent Shoots

As your opponent shoots in for either a double or single leg, you want to stop him with your forearm across his collarbone on one side and your hand on his shoulder or arm on the other side (f). You need to sprawl your legs back slightly. If you don't sprawl them back at all, he will usually get enough control of your legs to stop you from doing the move. If you sprawl back too far (g), you will have countered his shot but you will be out of position to spin behind him. It is best if you don't stop him completely, but continue his momentum forward by pulling his head down and his arm forward. You want to be able to get him down to at least his elbow (h) or better yet, flat on his chest. Once he's in this position, spin around as just described.

e

f

g

h

SHORT OFFENSE FROM AN ARM AND COLLAR TIE-UP

In the basic position, your right forearm is across your opponent's left collarbone. Your right hand can be free or around his head as a "collar," and your left arm is controlling his right arm.

Ankle or Knee Pick

Two short offense moves that can be done from an arm and collar tie-up, the ankle pick and the knee pick, have already been described. See pages 58 and 60.

Head-Snap on the Mat

Use your right forearm on his left collarbone to drive into him, shifting his weight back onto his feet and getting the weight off his hands (a). If he is not pushing back into you at all, you can take him directly over backward. He will usually push back into you, and as he does, use both hands to snap his head and arm forward and down to the mat where your right knee was (b). (Your knee won't be there because as you start to snap him down, you should also start spinning around him.)

a

b

Headlock

Drive into your opponent as just described for the start of the head-snap to get his weight shifted back, as shown above in *a*. Then throw your right arm past his head, as if you were trying to punch somebody two feet behind him, so that his head ends up under your shoulder. At the same time, use your left hand to pull his right arm forward. Don't headlock him straight over his right knee, which could act as a brace, but toward the front where he has no brace. Finish with any of the finishes described in the upcoming *Mat Finishes to a Headlock* section (pp. 108–109). The headlock can also be set up with the quarter nelson (page 40).

Shuck or Shrug

This move can be done starting in the position shown in photo *a*, above, and if so is called a *shuck*. The move is easier if your opponent has his left hand on your head and you are over his arm and locked around his head, in which case it is called a *shrug* (a, next page).

In this move, you are taking your opponent's head the opposite way as you did with a head-snap run-around. You use power from your shoulder plus the direct force of your hand and forearm on his head and neck to snap his head away from you. At the same time, reach your left arm over to help grab his left arm. You need to turn his body a little to clear his arm (b, next page), and then you can spin around him.

This move can be done just after you've stopped one of his shots and he's on his knees. Another good time is after you've tried to snap his head down and he counters by popping it back up. You can also use the head shuck as a set-up for the head-snap: If you shuck him but don't turn him enough to get around him, use his momentum to snap him down as he brings his head back.

a

b

SHORT OFFENSE FROM AN UNDERHOOK CONTROL

Instead of using your forearm to block your opponent's right collarbone, you can also counter him by underhooking the right side and blocking his left shoulder. You end up with his head under your chest and your legs back far enough so that he cannot reach them. For better power and mobility, be up on at least one foot, if not both.

Pancake

It is very difficult to pancake someone directly over a knee that he has out for a brace. Instead, pull your opponent's arm forward, which extends him, gets him off his brace, and helps clear his head (a and b). Rather than grabbing his right arm, it can be easier to clear his head if you control his right wrist and pull that forward. Clearing his head means getting it out from under your chest and left arm. To help you clear his head, use your chest to push his head to the left, away from your underhook, prior to hitting the pancake.

a

b

You can still pancake him if you don't clear his head, but his head ends up on top of your arm (c). It is much more difficult to hold him here because he usually spins right through before you obtain enough control for the takedown.

c

Pancake to the Spin-Around

If you try the pancake but your opponent does not go completely over to his back but only down to one shoulder or elbow (d), pull your right arm out and spin around his left side since his shoulder is down on that side. Use your left arm to block his right arm as you spin.

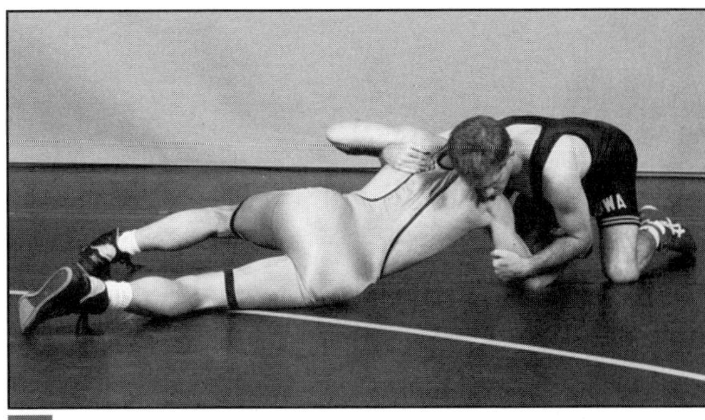

d

Knee Tap

Use your underhook arm to reach across underneath your opponent to block or "tap" the outside of his left knee or thigh. The palm of your hand should be against his knee or thigh with your thumb down (see photo). Come up on your feet and drive him over that knee. If you can, drive him all the way to his side or back and use your left arm to come underneath his right arm to keep him on his back. If you only block him down flat, spin around as described for the pancake.

Shuck

Come up on both toes and start running your opponent in a circle away from the underhook (right) side. Then unhook your underhook arm so your forearm is along the side of his face or neck (a), and shuck him in the same direction you are spinning him (b).

a

b

SHORT OFFENSE FROM A DOUBLE OVERHOOK

Spin-Around

If you are over both of your opponent's arms, it is hard to spin around him since he can lift either arm up to block you as you attempt to spin. However, if you pull him forward, this shifts his weight to his hands so he cannot react as quickly to you when you spin around. As you spin, you need to block his left arm as discussed for the *Head-Snap Run-Around* (page 89).

Knee Tap

If you are over your opponent's arm instead of under it, it is harder to reach his far knee; it is easier if you get off your knees and up on your toes.

Shuck

If you are running around your opponent's right side trying to reach his right leg for a cradle but he keeps spinning with you, use his momentum and your right arm to shuck him to his right.

Sit-Through

If you can lock your arms tight enough, you can sit your right leg through (a), taking your opponent over to his back. If you don't adjust your arms, you end up as shown in photo *b*. Or, as you roll through, you can release your left arm and come into a headlock position.

a

b

FRONT HEADLOCK DOWN ON THE MAT

The front headlock is a tie-up that traps one of your opponent's arms along his head, as in a headlock, except that you are in front of your opponent. The various takedowns that can be done from this tie-up will be discussed first for on the mat and then for up on the feet.

Basic Front Headlock

There are a couple of different ways to control the front headlock. One is to be over your opponent's head with your left arm and around his left arm with your right arm. Use your left forearm to turn his head toward his left arm (a and b). Make sure that you have either his left arm extended forward or your left elbow up high so that he cannot grab it with his left arm and do a short drag out of it (page 99). Your right arm should be pulling your opponent's left arm forward and have it tight to his head. You can either lock your hands or keep them unlocked and control his head and arm separately. You should be on your toes, your head should be on the side of his left shoulder, and your left shoulder should be on top of his left shoulder.

Another good front headlock position is to have your left shoulder on the back of his neck (to have downward pressure on his head) and with your right arm pull his elbow up (c).

a

b

Front Headlock From a Wizzer or an Underhook

■ *From a Wizzer.* If your opponent shot in on your legs and you countered with a wizzer on the right, square your hips and keep the wizzer in as an overhook. That right arm becomes the arm that controls his left arm, and then come over his head with your left arm to lock up the front headlock.

■ *From an Underhook.* If you counter your opponent's shot by underhooking his right arm with your left arm, use your chest to drive his head to the mat. Your left arm then becomes the arm around his head, and you can reach around his left arm with your right arm to get into the front headlock. Or, once you've driven his head down to the mat, you can bring your right arm around his head, take your underhook (left) arm out, and reach around his right arm with it.

c

REMEMBER—
It is illegal to have a front headlock without including an arm.

FINISHES FROM DOWN ON THE MAT

Shuck

Get up on your toes and run toward your opponent's left (where his arm is trapped, and therefore has no post) (photo *c*, page 95). Sometimes it is possible to run around him far enough to grab his left ankle to get control. If he is turning with you and you can't get around him, use his momentum and your left forearm to throw him by (see photo). Your legs have to be back far enough so that he doesn't catch them with his right arm.

Shuck the Opposite Way

If your opponent reaches up with his left arm to grab your left elbow and resists your efforts to spin him (a), you can shuck him back in the opposite direction (b).

a

b

Near-Side Cradle

Circle toward your opponent's trapped (left) arm. As he tries to circle with you, he will often bring his left knee up. If he does, keep control of his head with your left arm, but with your right arm reach behind his knee. Put your head in his side to help crunch him up, then lock your hands (see photo). Finish using any of the near-side cradle finishes (see chapter 4, page 160).

Grabbing His Ankle

If you circle around your opponent and he does not bring his knee up, but you can grab his ankle, do so. At the same time put your head into his side to block his left arm so he can't grab your left leg. With your left hand, grab his chin and pull it up and out (see photo). With the combination of your head in his side, twisting his head, and pulling his foot and leg out, he will usually go flat and let you run around him. If he tries instead to turn into you and brings his left knee up, cradle him as just described.

Knee Tap

The move is essentially the same as that described in the Knee Tap section of the Short Offense moves (see page 93). Use your left arm to reach across and block your opponent's knee.

★ Roll-Through

This is a good freestyle move, but it can also be used in scholastic wrestling. It is important to have your opponent locked up tight. Sit your right leg under your left leg (a) and roll through, bridging on your head (b). In freestyle, you may want to roll through two or more times to score additional back points. In scholastic wrestling, you should scissors your legs as you are coming out of the roll to come up on top of him (c).

a

b

c

Roll Through the Other Side

You can also roll through toward your opponent's free arm. It is more difficult, though, and you must be pulling his left arm forward so that he can't reach around your waist (d and e).

d

e

Pancake or Headlock

If your opponent is really fighting to get his head up, let go with your left arm and let him raise his head up. Use your now free left arm to hit a pancake (come under his right arm) or a headlock. Throughout the move, keep control of his left arm with your right arm.

Block His Arm With Your Leg

Step your left leg up so your knee is blocking his left arm, as shown in the photo. Unlock your arms and spin around him.

Head Chancery

"In chancery" refers to a hopeless predicament, and that is exactly the situation the head chancery puts your opponent in. Push his left elbow in to make him react by pushing it out. When he does, pull it out, duck your head underneath that arm, and keep your left arm around his head (see photo). Pull down on his head, lift up with your head, and grab and lift his left leg. You can finish with a cradle or a half nelson.

Ankle Pick

If your opponent is up off his knees, spin him toward his right foot. Just as he steps his left foot forward, use your right arm to pick his left ankle (see photo). If he counters by stepping that leg back, use your shoulder to keep his head blocked and use your right hand to do either an ankle pick or a knee block back to the right side.

COUNTER TO THE FRONT HEADLOCK DOWN ON THE MAT

If your opponent's arms are locked, do a short drag by bringing your "trapped" right arm up to hook his right arm (a), then pulling it through, ducking your head, and using your left arm to help throw him by you (b). This is hard to do if he has your right arm extended and tight to your head, and is nearly impossible if he doesn't have his arms locked but instead is holding your right arm out separately (see photo *a* on page 95).

Counter to the Short Drag

The counter to the short drag is good positioning. If somehow you get out of position and you feel your opponent starting to arm drag you (a), you can shift your head to the side of his free arm (c).

a

b

c

FRONT HEADLOCK FROM THE FEET

If he wrestles with his head down, tie-up with head and arm control, then snap his head down and change to the front headlock. Or, use a right underhook to pull his head and shoulders down, and then reach over his head with your left arm. Change your right arm from an underhook to an overhook, locking around his left arm. In either case, have your hands locked in the same way they were when you were down on the mat, as shown.

Finishes From the Feet

Once locked up on the feet, you can sprawl your legs back, bringing your opponent down to the mat, and use any of the finishes just covered. Or you can stay up on your feet and use any of the finishes described here.

★*Fireman's Carry*

Circle your opponent to his left side. As he steps forward with his right foot, release his left arm, drop your head and right shoulder underneath his arm, and reach around his right knee. Use your left arm to control his chin (a). Go down to your knees (b) and finish as with any fireman's carry (see pp. 76–80).

Knee Pick

Start as for the *Fireman's Carry*, but rather than dropping under your opponent and lifting him, drive straight through him.

a

b

Opposite Knee Pick

You can also attack the left leg: Circle to his right to get him stepping his left leg toward you. Keep his head blocked as you reach with your left arm behind his knee (c) or ankle, and drive into him.

Inside Trip

Pull your opponent toward you and as he is stepping his left leg forward, step in with your right leg to inside trip his left leg (d).

c

d

TWO-ON-ONE

The two-on-one is a tie-up in which you hold one of your opponent's arms with both of your arms. This tie-up not only negates much of your opponent's offense, but it can also be used to set up many different takedowns.

Basic Two-on-One

The most frequent opportunity for getting into the two-on-one occurs when your opponent has a head tie-up. Reach up with your left arm and grab his left wrist (a). Use your right shoulder and forearm to help take his arm off your head. After you pull his wrist off your head, use your right arm to hold his arm in tight to your chest, and use your head to block his head (b).

a

b

If he gets his head to the inside so he is blocking your head, shrug your shoulder into him to clear his head (c), and then return to the correct position. Once you have his arm controlled, an additional adjustment you can make that allows you to extend his elbow and sag on his arm more effectively is to change the grip with your left hand so that your palm faces forward instead of back (d).

c

d

TWO-ON-ONE FINISHES

Drag

Change your left hand from controlling your opponent's wrist to controlling his arm (see photo). Then use your left arm to drag him forward as you slide your right arm around his waist. At the same time you should step your left knee across his front to block him so he can't run by you.

Snatch Single Leg

Keep control of the two-on-one as you pull your opponent's arm down toward his left leg, as shown. Once you've driven his arm to his knee, let go of the arm and do a snatch single leg (a).

Step on His Toe (Single)

Another way of getting into the single leg is to step on your opponent's left toe before driving his arm toward his leg, making it more difficult for him to step his leg back.

Hook His Leg (Single)

Alternatively, you can hook his left leg with your right leg, and then change to a single leg (b).

a

b

Double

If your opponent puts his right hand on your head or shoulder (a), use his left arm to hit his right arm above his elbow, driving it up and clearing his legs (b). If you hit his right arm below his elbow, he can just bend his elbow, and you won't clear his arm. Don't release his left arm until you have completely penetrated.

You can also attempt a double leg by starting the drag as described above. If you cannot get him by enough to get behind him for control, but get enough of an angle on him, shoot a double leg (without going down to your knees) with your head to the outside of his left hip.

Bear Hug

Use the same set-up as in the double, but lock your arms around his waist rather than around his legs.

a

b

★ Fireman's Carry

Your opponent needs to be squared up in front of you for you to throw this move. He may position himself in front of you trying to get out of the two-on-one. Another way of getting him to square up to you is to drive your shoulder into him (see *Basic Two-on-One*, photo *c*, page 102), or reach for his left leg to get him to step it back. Once he is squared up (a) or, better, *as* he is squaring up, keep control of his arm with your right arm but let go of his wrist with your left hand and use that arm to reach between his legs as you step in for the fireman's carry (page 76).

a

b

Fireman's With the Arm Only

The move is set up just as with a regular fireman's carry. It helps to twist your opponent's forearm in (so his palm is facing out) to lock his arm. Then, step into the fireman's position (b), and finish by driving through at about a 45-degree angle (c). You can use your left forearm and elbow to help throw him over. Control his arm throughout the entire move.

c

Don't turn after you have penetrated and try to finish by taking him at a 90-degree angle to he direction you shot in, since he is likely to sag back on you and you will lose control. As with all fireman's carries, it is very important to pull his left arm down tight so that his left shoulder is tight to your right shoulder.

Near-Arm Far-Leg

Set up your opponent as for the fireman's carry, but instead of reaching for his left leg, reach across for his right leg with your left arm. Be sure to pull his head and left shoulder down with you.

Knee Trip

Release your left arm but continue tight control of your opponent's left arm with your right arm and have your shoulder pressure across his arm. Reach your left arm across to block his right knee, as shown, and then use your shoulder pressure to drive into him.

Ankle Pick or Ankle Block

Ankle Pick

Step your right thigh in to lift your opponent's left leg, shifting his weight to his right leg (a). As you bring your right foot down, place it behind his right ankle, blocking it (see page 58). You may be able to drive him over that ankle without letting go of his wrist or arm, or you may need to let go of his wrist and grab his ankle with your left hand. As with all ankle picks, take his head down toward his ankle.

Ankle Block

Hang heavy on your opponent's arm and circle in front of him. Use your right leg to block and lift his left ankle as you continue to circle away by hopping on your left foot (b).

a

b

Arm Throw

Circle in front of your opponent, and as he starts to follow you (not after he has already closed the gap), bend your knees and lower your right shoulder so that your shoulder is under his left arm and your right hip is under his hip. Then, straighten your knees, holding his arm tight to your chest, and complete the throw, as shown.

If He Reaches Over Your Head or Across to Grab Your Elbow

If your opponent is reaching across to grab your elbow (a), try a double leg or a headlock.

Double Leg

Do essentially the same move as if he reached for your head or shoulder (see the *Double*, photos *a* and *b*, page 103).

Headlock

Release his wrist with your left hand and grab his right arm just above the elbow. Then use your right arm to throw the headlock (b).

Over Your Head

If he's reaching over your head (c), keep his arm tight, block his left ankle with your right foot, and sit (d), bringing him down to the mat.

a

b

c

d

COUNTERS TO THE TWO-ON-ONE

High Crotch

The best defense is to keep your opponent from getting the two-on-one and to gain a takedown in the same process. As he is just starting to take your hand off of his head to get into the two-on-one, hit a high crotch (a).

Grab His Elbow

As just explained, if you try to grab your opponent's elbow, he could do a double leg or headlock (page 105). This can be avoided if at the same time you squat (b) to get your head to the inside of his, which makes it difficult for him to get back into good position.

Step Behind His Leg

The third counter is to squat, step behind your opponent's left leg, and hook it (c). You can then limp arm out (d), and, if possible, grab his left leg for a single leg. Alternatively, you can go down to your right knee as you do this.

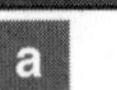

a

b

c

d

HEADLOCK

This is a throw that starts and finishes with control of your opponent's head and one of his arms. A tight headlock truly does "lock" his head and is an effective pinning combination.

★Basic Headlock

From a head and arm tie-up, step your right foot across to your opponent's right foot. You can accomplish the same thing by making him come to you—that is, use your right hand on his head to jerk him behind you. Then, backstep (described in the Basic Skills section, page 4) to get your left hip all the way through (this is the key part of the move) and throw your right arm past his head so that his head ends up underneath your shoulder (a). As you backstep, your knees will be bent. Once your hips are through (b), straighten your legs and pull his right arm down to finish the throw (c).

b

c

d

He Has a Head Tie-Up

If your opponent ties up your head or shoulder with his right arm, reach over that arm with your left arm and either lock his forearm to your chest by pulling it in tight to you, or, if you can, grab the inside of his elbow. Backstep your hips through (b).

Pummeling

Just after you have changed from an underhook to an overhook on your opponent's right side, trap his right forearm against your chest. Then, as you are changing from an underhook to an overhook on his left side, use your right arm to hit the headlock.

Locked Around His Arm and Head

You can get into this position in two ways:

- *From a Bear Hug.* From a bear hug position, with your arms locked around your opponent's back under his right arm and over his left one, slide both arms up so you are around his head with his right arm pinched to the side of his head (d). Ideally, you can do a headlock in a continuous motion—that is, slide up from the bear hug to around his head and continue stepping through to do the head-lock.
- *Starting With an Underhook.* You can also get into this position by starting with an underhook with your left arm. Reach around your opponent's head with your right arm and lock your hands. You should try to raise his right arm so it is alongside his head.

Two-on-One

See *Headlock* in the Two-on-One section, page 105.

He Has a Bear Hug

See the Bear Hug section on page 88 (photo *a*).

FINISHES FROM THE FEET WHEN LOCKED AROUND HIS ARM AND HEAD

Headlock

Jerk your opponent to his left first, then when he reacts and pulls back, backstep in and throw the headlock to the other side (a, next page).

Headlock and Block

From the locked position, step your right leg behind your opponent's right leg so that you are blocking above and behind his knee (b, next page). As you step, you want all your weight to be driving over his. Lift his leg as you drive.

a

b

Finish if You Miss or Slip Off His Head

Keep your hip and arm momentum going, and keep tight control of your opponent's right arm. Hook his right elbow with your right arm (a) and take him to the mat (b). Once you've taken him to the mat, you can either keep his arm and adjust your back pressure to his chest to try to hold him on his back, or you can change to a headlock position.

a

b

MAT FINISHES TO A HEADLOCK

When you land, continue holding your opponent's right arm and post with your right arm so he can't roll you through (page 110, photo *b*). Once you've landed and adjusted your weight, you can put your right arm around his head again. Your legs should be out perpendicular to his body. There are at least four ways you can finish from here:

Lift His Head Up

Pull up on your opponent's head and arm so he can't bridge (a).

a

b

Arm Across His Face

Push your opponent's arm across his face, hold it there momentarily with your head (you need to be above his elbow), then lock your hands (b).

Hips Down

Get to the position shown in photo *b*, then scissor your right leg under your left leg so that you turn your hips down. You can then drive your right shoulder up into your opponent (c). This can be a dangerous hold, as it's possible for your opponent to pass out.

Lift Elbow

Bring your left arm underneath your opponent's right arm and elbow and lift both his elbow and his head (d).

c

d

ALTERNATIVES TO THE HEADLOCK IF YOU DON'T GET YOUR HIPS THROUGH

If you couldn't get your hips through, as shown, this may be because you didn't do an adequate backstep or because your opponent stepped his right hip in to block you. In either case, your options are a restep, a sag step, or a block and trip.

Restep

Simply reverse your backstep. This not only gets you out of danger but also sets up a headlock. Immediately after you have stepped out, your opponent will usually be relaxed and you can step back in.

a

b

c

Sag Step

Continue to pull your opponent's right arm tight across your chest. Put more pressure on his head by rotating your right forearm inward so that your palm is facing back. At the same time, take a big step with your right foot, sagging all of your weight on his head (a). Post your right arm out so you can't be rolled through (b).

Block and Trip

You can step your right leg around your opponent's right leg (c) and do the throw as described under *Headlock and Block*, pages 107–108.

COUNTERS TO THE HEADLOCK

Here are three of the best ways to counter a headlock, plus a last resort:

Duck Your Head

As soon as you feel a headlock coming, duck your head, shrug your shoulders up, and use your right hand to push your opponent's arm over your head.

Hip Block

Step your hips into your opponent as he tries to get his hips through, and squat so that your hips are lower than his (a). He should not be able to do a headlock if he does not get his hips through, although he does have the alternatives described in the previous section. Try to drive his arm over your head so that he cannot accomplish any of these alternative finishes.

Back Throw

After you stop your opponent from getting his hips all the way through and you have your hips lower than his, as just described, step your left foot in front of him, pull his hips tight in to yours, then do a back arch to take him over (b).

a

b

Roll

If you missed the opportunity to do any of the previous counters and you are on your way down to your back, lock your hands around your opponent's body and pull him tight to you (keeping his body as parallel to your body as possible). As you hit, keep his momentum going and bridge on your head as you take him over to his back.

SHOULDER THROWS

The various shoulder throws involve attacking your opponent's shoulder either by levering underneath it (in the standing and kneeling shoulder throws) or by driving into it using the shoulder hit.

Standing Shoulder Throw

Start with either an over-underhook (an overhook on your opponent's left side) or your head and arm control controlling his left arm. Pull him toward his right, then release your left arm (from either his head or the underhook depending on what tie-up you started with) and reach your arm across to hook and control his left arm (a). Pull his left shoulder tight into your chest with both of your arms. Either at the same time or just after you have reached your left arm across, backstep to his left to get your hips all the way through. You end up with your opponent's arm draped over your arm (you don't want his arm to slip above your shoulder). From here, straighten your legs, pull down on his arm, and throw him just as you would with a hip toss or headlock (b).

a

b

Kneeling Shoulder Throw

Start the move just as you would for the standing shoulder throw, but after you have backstepped, go down on both your knees. It is extremely important to keep your opponent's left shoulder and arm pulled tight into you. Continue to pull him over you as you take him to his back.

Shoulder Hit

Unlike the other two shoulder throws just described, in this one you are *not* going to get your hips through. Start the move as you would for the standing shoulder throw, that is, with the same choices of tie-up and by circling him toward his right. As you bring your left arm across, do not just hook his left arm, but also hit and drive your left shoulder into his shoulder. By circling him first, you should be able to get an angle on him so that you are driving into him at right angles to his base.

Continue to drive your opponent down to the mat, keeping his arm tight to your chest the whole way (a).

a

Shoulder Hit Finishes

There are three finish options:

- *Pancake Position.* Release your left arm as soon as you hit and come across your opponent's chest and under his right arm.
- *Headlock Position.* Bring your left arm around his head for a headlock.
- *Back-to-Chest Finish.* Keep your opponent's arm tight to your chest and turn your back on top of his chest (b).You should be able to hold him there long enough to get control for a takedown plus back points.

The first two finish options give you more control, but it can be difficult to get your left arm out in time to get it across your opponent's chest before he starts to come behind you. Even after he has started to come behind you, you can still do the back-to-chest finish.

b

3

Escapes and Reversals

To be a successful wrestler, you must be able to get away from any opponent. Even if you can't ride or pin someone, if you can take him down and escape or reverse him without first giving up back points, you can't be beat! Most wrestlers have more fun working on takedowns than on mat wrestling, but we can't stress enough that you must devote time and effort to becoming an expert at getting away.

An *escape* is scored when the bottom wrestler gets free—to the neutral position. A *reversal* occurs when the bottom wrestler "reverses" positions and goes from being controlled to controlling his opponent. Depending on what finish you use and how your opponent reacts, you can execute the same move to score either an escape or a reversal.

A few basic principles apply to almost all escapes and reversals. First is to work from a good base. You can do very little when you're flat on your stomach, so whenever you get broken down you should get back to your base (page 4). Second, realize that you don't need to be completely broken down before you start to get away. All too often a wrestler taken down will go flat to his stomach, swear at himself, look at the coach, try to figure out what happened, and then—if he isn't already on his back—finally try to get to his base and get out. Instead, *as* you are being taken down or broken down, you should already be starting to escape. If an opponent has you three quarters of the way taken down you should consider yourself one quarter of the way *out*—and therefore already working to get totally out before you are totally taken down. As with all other positions, chain wrestling is important in escaping—if the first move doesn't work, immediately hit a second.

The third and most important basic principle for escapes and reversals is to always have hand control. Getting hand control should be the first step in almost every escape. Without it, good position, effort, and all subsequent moves may simply be wasted.

STAND-UPS

A stand-up is a move that takes you from the mat to the standing position. In the correct starting bottom stance, your elbows should be in and back toward your knees, as shown below. From this position, if your opponent chops your arm, your elbow will come back to your knee, making it difficult for him to arm-bar you.

There are two key points to the many types of stand-ups. First, get hand control before or as you start to come up. Don't come up to your feet first and then fight for hand control. Second, as you come up, drive your back *into* the man. Don't come up with your weight forward.

INCORRECT STANCE

Your elbows should not be out, because this makes it very easy for the top man to chop your left arm and arm-bar it.

Inside-Leg Stand-Up Catching the Wrist

As you step your inside (left) foot up and drive back into your opponent, throw your left arm up, reach under it with your right arm, and grab his left wrist (a). Next, drive your back into him and pivot up on your right foot, without taking a step with your right foot. As you are coming up, grab his left wrist with your right hand (b) and lock your left arm straight. (If your elbow is bent, a good opponent could overpower your and bring his arm back around your waist. But your locked elbow provides tremendous mechanical advantage. No opponent should be able to get his left hand back around your waist.) Have your left leg out in front of you, your right leg back, your back driving into him, and your hips out (c).

a

b

c

Both Hands to His Hand Around Your Waist

As in the previous stand-up, step your inside foot up and drive your back into your opponent. With both of your hands, grab his right hand. Your left arm and elbow should be tight to your side so that he cannot reach under with his left hand. Next, pivot back into him, coming to your feet. This gets you into essentially the same position as in the previous move (photo *c*, above), except you have control of his right rather than his left hand. If you keep your left arm tight to your side, your opponent must go over your left arm rather than under it (as shown in photo), which makes it harder for him to control you.

Inside-Leg Stand-Up Bringing Your Elbow Back

Step your inside foot up and drive back just as in the first stand-up. As you step up, drive your left elbow back into the opponent's chest and control the fingers of his right hand. Pivot up on the right foot, straighten your right arm, and finish as in the first stand-up.

Outside-Leg Stand-Ups

These can be done just as in any of the previous stand-ups, the only difference being that you first step up with your outside foot.

Feet-Out Stand-Up

If the top man is quick at picking the outside ankle (after he grabs it, he picks it up and drives forward), he can stop your inside-leg stand-up. One way to overcome this is to pivot on both knees and slide both feet to the outside as your initial move (a)—your knees don't move at all. The opponent can still easily pick your right ankle, but he will be extended more, and your having more weight on that ankle will make it nearly impossible for him to pick it up. As you pivot your feet out, reach back with your right hand to control his right wrist (b). Pull his right arm forward (to keep your chest tight to him), and drive back into him to come to your feet (c). Never take a step with your feet; initially you pivot on your knees to get your feet out, then you plant your feet and push back into him. If you get space between your back and his chest he could possibly suck you back underneath him. If on your way up he tries to set you on your butt, you can hip-heist toward his left (page 2).

a

b

c

He Has Your Outside Ankle

This move is very similar to the feet-out stand-up. Drive your weight back over your feet, putting you into a solid base and making it difficult for your opponent to pick your ankle up. Reach back with your right hand and grab his wrist as you rotate back over your right foot (your right knee will come up). The rest of the move is as just described for the *Feet-Out Stand-Up*.

Short Sit Directly to a Stand-Up

From a short sit-out, with both feet close to your butt and planted on the mat, control the hand that is around your waist, keeping your left elbow in so the opponent can't reach under it. By pulling his right arm forward, pushing it down toward your hip, and driving back into him, you will come up to your feet. Turn his head away by driving your head into it. You can either come all of the way up to your feet or hip-heist out at any level. If he is able to pull you back as you are coming up, you should definitely hip-heist out.

From a Short Sit-Out, Post Your Hand

You are in a sit-out position with your left arm to your side so that your opponent can't come underneath it. He has his right hand around your waist, and your right hand is posted on the mat. Bring your right knee back underneath you (a). This puts him perpendicular to you on the side where he has an underhook, so he can't chop you down until he spins around to your left side, where he is over your arm. As your opponent starts to spin around you, push back into him, and get control of either wrist as you come to your feet (b).

a

b

FINISHES TO THE STAND-UP ONCE YOU ARE ON YOUR FEET

Turn

From the standing position, with control of your opponent's left wrist, your left foot in front of you, your back turned into the opponent, and your butt out (photo *c*, page 114), simply step your right foot behind your left foot, as shown. Control his left hand until you are facing him. As you turn, don't worry about the hand that is around your waist. As long as you turn into it, he can't hold you with it. It is important to have your hands in front of you once you have faced him so that you are ready to block him in case he is shooting in.

THE WRONG TURN

Turning *with* your opponent's grip around your waist rather than turning *into* it will tighten the grip. It is possible to get out this way but you must create significant space between your hips and his.

Shear

In this finish, your arm comes down over the opponent's shoulder as if shearing it. From the same standing position described in the last move, raise your right arm so it is along the side of your head. Step your right leg behind your left leg, slide your hips down, and bring your arm down between his shoulder and head, as shown, *not* over his arm. This is not a power move. You are simply sliding away from him.

If He Is Behind You With His Hands Locked, to Break His Grip . . .

Attack the Bottom Wrist

Grab your opponent's bottom wrist with your hands (a) and push it down to your left hip. Fight him two hands on one, not one on one. As you drive his hands down to your hip, throw your back into him and your hips out, breaking his grip.

Attack His Top Hand

Attack your opponent's top hand by cupping under his thumb and turning his hand up and out (b). From here, arch your hips out and throw your back into him as just described.

Attack His Forearms

If your opponent's hands are up around your chest, you can drive both of your elbows back against his forearms. At the same time arch your hips out and your back into him.

If you can't break his grip . . .

Escape With a Switch

If you are going to switch to your opponent's right side, you want to have his right leg back so that there is space between your hips and his. You can do this by walking forward and hitting the switch just as his right leg is ready to follow forward but has not stepped yet. Or, you can fake a switch to the left side and then hit the switch to the right. When you do switch, drive your elbow down hard on his right arm, reach for the inside of his right leg, and get your hips away from him (c). You can go down to the mat or stay on your feet to finish.

Escape With an Ankle Block

Grab your opponent's right wrist with your left hand. Walk forward so that he has to follow you, and just as he plants his right foot, post your right foot to the outside of it as a block (d). Then, holding his arm tight across your waist (pulling his hips tight to yours), throw your hips down to the mat. After you both hit the mat, you can switch hands and come into a Peterson or turn toward his legs to gain control.

a

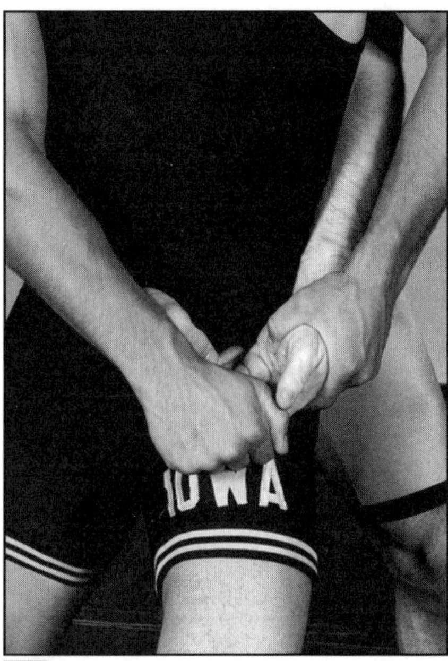

b

c

d

Escape With a Standing Peterson

As with the switch, you need to create some space between your hips and your opponent's right thigh since you are going to be trying to get your hips through. Step your left leg between your right leg and his, controlling his right wrist with your right hand and reaching between his legs with your left arm and grabbing his right leg (e). From here, roll down to your right hip first (f) and then into the Peterson position (g).

If you get your hips all the way through and control your opponent's arm tightly around your waist, you can also do essentially the same move without reaching between his legs. After you roll him to his back, change to the Peterson position.

Escape With a Standing Granby

Similar to down on the mat, a granby can be done from the standing position. It is described in the Granbys section (page 138).

e

f

g

COUNTERS TO THE STAND-UP FINISHES

In general, you want to keep your opponent's hips tight into yours and keep your hips lower than his, as shown. This eliminates much of his offense. The following moves are used when you are locked around his waist without either of his arms locked. However, if you can lock one of his arms, you will have more control and these finishes will be easier.

Step to His Side and Lift

Step around your opponent's left side with your knees bent so your hips are below his. Ideally you will be able to get around his side enough so that you will be straddling his leg and be perpendicular to him. Without stopping your momentum, explode your hips into him and lift him with your legs (not your back). In freestyle or Greco-Roman, you can continue backward and throw him to his back (page 110). In scholastic wrestling, to avoid getting called for a slam, it is probably best to use the lift just to get his legs off the mat and then take him down forward.

Fake Stepping to One Side and Then Going to the Opposite Side

When you try stepping around your opponent's left side, he will often step his left leg forward to keep you from getting your leg in front of his. If he does this, you can fake stepping to the left side (step only enough to get him to step his left leg forward) and then take a long step around to his right side so you are straddling that leg. Finish as just described.

Outside Trip

Step your right leg around your opponent's right leg and at the same time unlock your hands and grab his left thigh with your left hand. As you trip him forward, use your left arm to pull his hips through. Finish just as you do with the jam breakdown (page 139, photo *b*)—setting him on his butt in front of you. Make sure your head is up and your hand is on his hip, not around his waist; otherwise, he could switch you.

Outside Trip With Other Leg

Step your left leg and hip in front of your opponent's right leg and pull him down over your leg, as shown. This move is much easier if you have control of his right arm.

Inside Trip

Bend your knees, lower your hips, step your left leg around his right leg, as shown, and trip him forward.

Snap-Back

If your opponent is standing straight up, lift him up and throw your hips into him to get his legs out. Then unlock your hands and come underneath both of his arms (a). Hook your chin over his shoulder as you pull him down to the mat (b).

a

b

Sag on Thigh

Bring your locked hands over to the front of your opponent's right thigh. Pry the bony (outside) part of your forearm down on his thigh. You should be able to get enough pressure to take him down on that side.

Sweeping His Legs

From directly behind your opponent, lift him so that his weight is off his feet. Bend your right knee and sweep his legs up and out by sweeping his right leg at a point above his knee, as shown.

Ankle Block

Step your right foot up to block the back of your opponent's right foot and shift your hips so that you are tight to his left hip, as shown. Keep your hips tight to him throughout the entire move and pull him backward in a circular motion. He should land on his butt, not on you. If you allow space between your hips and his as you pull him back, he could switch you as you are going back or after you hit the mat.

Leg Tackle

If the opponent has broken your grip and is about to turn to get loose, lower your hips, release your hands from around his waist, and then grab him just below his knees. The drive your shoulder into the back of his thighs, as shown.

Shooting in on a Single

If your opponent has freed his hands and is turning to face you, shoot in for a double or single leg just as he is turning. Don't wait until he has turned and has a good stance.

Crotch Lift

If your opponent has broken your grip and has control of one of your hands out to his side (a), bring that hand behind him and through his crotch (b) while keeping the other hand around his waist. From here you can lift him and take him to the mat.

a

b

Bear Hug

This move is described in the *Bear Hugs* section (page 86).

SIT-OUTS

This series of moves includes a variety of escapes and reversals that all require getting to a sitting position. Although some of the moves involve sitting back or in rather than out, they are all grouped under the term *sit-out*.

Short Sit-Out

In a short sit-out, the sitting motion is short, placing you immediately in front of your opponent. From the referee's position, post on your left hand and simultaneously sit both legs in front of you. Use your right hand to control his fingers or wrist (a).

a

You will end up on your butt with both legs out in front of you and your opponent behind you (b). Your butt should be right under your shoulders—you shouldn't be leaning too far forward with your head near your knees since he could cradle you. You also should not be leaning back since he could pull you down to your shoulders. If he does try to pull your shoulders back, scoot your butt underneath you. Your knees should be bent and your feet planted on the mat so you can push off of them. With your right arm you will be controlling his wrist or fingers and your left arm should be tight to your side so that he cannot reach under.

b

Ways to finish a short sit-out . . .

Sit-and-Turn

Keeping control of your opponent's right hand, go down to your left shoulder (not your elbow), pulling his arm from around your waist to up underneath your armpit so he can't follow you as easily. As your shoulder is going down to the mat, your right knee should be coming up to your head (a). Try to stay as tight as possible. If you go down to your shoulder to turn but do not follow with your right knee, he could pull you to your back. The tighter you turn, the better. Imagine that there is a string tied between your head and your right knee. As soon as your head and shoulder start to go down to the left, your right knee should follow and at no time should the distance between your head and your knee be more than it is in the sit-out position. Control his right hand throughout the entire move. Once you have turned in, you can pop your head and left arm out and come around behind him (b).

a

b

Hook-and-Turn

If you are in the sitting position and your opponent puts either his head or his left arm over your shoulder, hook it with your left arm and turn the opposite way (c).

c

Turn Toward His Head

Even if your opponent is not hanging his head over your shoulder, you can frequently hook his head as you do this move. Post on your left arm, duck your head, and bring your left knee back underneath you (d). Throw your right arm over your head (e), try to pop your left arm out the back, and either come around behind him or take him directly to his back if possible.

★Peterson

This is a finish that can be used initially or as a salvage move if you did a sit-and-turn and wanted to pop out behind your opponent but couldn't get your head and shoulders all the way out. As with the sit-and-turn, keep control of his right wrist throughout the move. Pull it tight up under your arm pit, and with your left arm reach between his legs and grab his right leg (f). Continue to turn as you look back toward your feet. Finish by rolling him to his back (g). (See photo *g*, page 119.) The Peterson also works well if you are doing a sit-and-turn and he is following you.

Roll

As with the Peterson, this works well when your opponent is following you as you are completing the sit-and-turn. As he follows you, pull his right arm tight around your waist, put your left hand on the inside of his left leg, and try to throw his left leg over your back (h). Control his wrist with your right arm. As long as you pull his wrist tight around your waist, you do not need to hook his elbow with your right arm.

Other Ways to Finish the Short Sit-Out

- *Hip Heist*—see the upcoming Hip Heist section (page 129);
- *Stand-up*, see the Stand-Up section (page 116);
- *Granby*, see the upcoming Granbys section (pp. 137–138).

d

e

f

g

h

Sit-Back

This sit move differs from the sit-out because rather than sitting in front of your opponent, you are sitting back into him. The goal is actually to sit on top of him. Your feet don't really change position—you pivot on the toes of your left foot and push off with your right foot. Control his right hand, which is around your waist, as you sit back on top of him. The move is shown without the opponent on top of you (a and b) and the position that you will typically get into when an opponent is riding you (c). By pushing on top of him, you should be driving him to his butt, where he cannot follow you as easily. From this position, pull his right hand up into your armpit, turn down onto your left shoulder, and turn tightly as described previously (page 124).

a

b

c

★ Inside Sit

This move feels very awkward when you are learning it, and is markedly different than any other sit-out. However, if mastered, it will be your fastest escape. It is a two-step move, first turning back into your opponent and then doing a short turn in the opposite direction, but it is done as one continuous move between the two steps.

The initial move is to just raise your left (inside) knee up as you sit on your right hip. Your left arm drives back into the opponent. The combination of driving your back into him, raising your left knee, and driving your left arm into him drives him behind you rather than on your side. If you keep your left arm next to your chest, he will usually overhook your arm (a), but even if he is under your arm the move will still work. Stay in that position only momentarily; as soon as you hit there, turn back in the opposite direction. Go down to your right shoulder (not your elbow) and drive your knee to your head (b and c). If he has overhooked your arm, throw that over your head as you turn, or if you can, grab his head.

a

b

c

Long Sit-Out

The long sit-out starts just like the short sit-out—posting on your left hand and then swinging your legs out in front of you. But with the long sit-out, you kick your legs out in front of you as far as you can (a). Rather than landing on your butt, you land on your left side and hip (b). You finish by kicking your right leg over your left one, and facing your opponent.

a

b

COUNTERS TO THE SIT-OUT

We'll describe counters to the sit-out from two situations: when your opponent is stationary and sitting in front of you, and when he is in the process of turning from a sit-out position.

Opponent is Stationary, Sitting in Front of You

Here are four good options for countering the sitting, stationary opponent:

Pry on His Thighs

Be up on your toes with your head directly behind your opponent's head and one (or both if possible) of your arms under his arms, prying on his thigh(s) (a). If you have both arms on his thighs, you can take him either to the left or to the right. If you can control one wrist, it is easier to turn him to that side since he can't post on that hand (b).

a

b

Drive His Head Between His Knees

Drive directly over your opponent, getting his head down at or between his knees. Keeping chest pressure on his back, grab his chin with your left hand and his right thigh with your right hand (c). Then come over to his right side and pull him back (d).

Cradle

Drive directly over your opponent as just described, getting his head down at his knees. Then slide quickly to either side and cradle him.

Suck-Back

If your opponent does not have his hips underneath him or if you can get him to push back into you (by pushing into him first), suck him back with double underhooks (e). With the double underhooks, it is hard to pin him, but you can usually hold him long enough to get back points. Alternatively, you can grab his chin with one of your underhook arms, and then pull him back.

c

d

e

Opponent is Turning From the Sit-Out

Try one of these countermoves for a turning opponent:

Follow in the Same Direction

If the opponent does not do a tight turn, it should be easy to follow behind him in the same direction he is turning. It is important to stay underneath his left arm so that he cannot grab you or roll you. Also, if possible, clear your legs to his other side, which will keep him from rolling or doing a Peterson on you.

Spin the Opposite Direction

If your opponent does a good turn to his left, and he is either already turned or you feel that if you attempt to follow him he will be able to roll or Peterson you, do the following: Post your right hand on the mat behind his right arm, as shown (if before he turned you were under his right arm, you should naturally be in this position). Then, as he is finishing his turn, spin around his right side.

HIP HEIST

The hip heist can be done from several positions, but the basic movement—scissoring your legs so that you change your hips from facing upward to downward—is the same. This was described from the referee's position in the Basic Skills section (page 2).

Sit-Out to a Hip Heist

From a short sit-out, control your opponent's right wrist and pull it forward so that you can drive back into him (a). If you drive back into him without grabbing his wrist, he can suck you back. Keep your left arm next to your side so that he cannot reach underneath it and around your waist. Once your hips are off the mat, do a hip heist (b). You don't want to end up just in front of the opponent but in front and away from him.

a

b

Sit-Out to a Stand-Up to a Hip Heist

If you have done a sit-out and are pushing back into your opponent to come up to your feet (page 116) but he sucks you back, you should do a hip heist. Alternatively, you can plan to do the hip heist at any level of the stand-up—that is, one-quarter of the way, one-half of the way, or completely up. The sit-out to a hip heist just described is essentially a hip heist at the very beginning of a stand-up. The movement is the same at all levels.

Switch to a Hip Heist

If you get your hips out in the switch position but can't complete the switch (a) (it may be because he has your left arm), you can hip-heist out by driving your right leg underneath your left leg (b).

a

b

Hip Heist to Counter a Double Leg

As soon as the opponent sits you on your butt, if your legs are to his right side, post your right arm and get your butt off the mat (a). Then, hit a hip heist from this position (scissors your right leg under the left one) (b).

It is easiest to do the hip heist just as you hit on your butt rather than after he has adjusted his weight and has a good grip. If his head is to your right side, post your right hand on his head rather than on the mat.

a

b

SWITCHES

When done properly, this move switches your position from underneath to on top. The various switches all involve turning back into your opponent and driving your arm over his arm and under his leg.

Switch From Referee's Position

Two things are done simultaneously as the switch is started. Raise your right knee up as you pivot on your outside foot and shift your left arm across (to get him extended). Sit your left leg through, plant it away from your opponent, and at the same time drive your right arm over his shoulder and then under his right leg (a). Don't sit back toward his legs with your hips parallel to his. You want to get your hips away from him and get him extended. Drive his right shoulder down to the mat (b) (and preferably drive his right arm off your waist so that he can't reswitch you) and then scissors your left leg over the right leg and go behind him.

a

b

Power Switch

You typically do not want your hips parallel to your opponent's when you switch. However, if you get into this position while scrambling, bend your knee and block his right side with it so he can't step across you. Hook your right foot under his thigh, grab under your knee with your right arm (a), and lift your leg to elevate him over (b).

a

b

Inside Switch

This move works best when your opponent is moving his left arm from your elbow to your waist (as he would do in going for an outside ankle pick). Lift your inside knee and step your right leg through at about a 45-degree angle, as shown. You want to get your hips away from him if you can and reach your left arm over his left shoulder and under his left thigh to switch him.

Short Sit to a Switch

If you get into a short sit-out position and your opponent keeps his arm around your waist (page 124, page top), you could do a routine switch over his right arm and under his right leg as just described. However, it can be difficult to get your arm under his thigh since you are more in front of him rather than turning back toward him. The other problem with a switch from this position is that if he does a limp-arm-out you will be in bad shape (page 132). Therefore, lock his right arm by grabbing it with your left arm and then switching.

SWITCH FROM A STAND-UP.
See Stand-Up Finishes, page 118, photo *c*

SWITCH TO A HIP HEIST.
See the Hip Heist section (page 129).

COUNTERS TO SWITCHES

Chop His Arm

If your opponent leaves his left arm behind him, or if he tries to bring it across but he doesn't do a good job of getting you extended, keep control of his elbow and pull it behind his back, then drive him down to his side as you hip into him.

Reswitch

As your opponent is just starting to come around on top of you (a), your right arm is already in position to do a switch on him (b). To make sure he doesn't reswitch you again, slide your hips away from him as you finish the switch so that his arm clears your waist.

Countering His Reswitch

If your opponent has done a reswitch but hasn't shifted his hips away to clear your arm from his waist, you can reswitch him. Whether he clears your arm or not, you can post on your head and step across both of his legs (c). This could also be tried to counter a switch but it is more difficult to get across both of his legs in that situation since his hips are usually further away from you.

a

b

c

Limp-Arm-Out

Pull your arm out from around your opponent's waist, thereby taking away all of his leverage. You need to do it before he has pressure down on your shoulder since by that time it is too late. Once you limp-arm-out you can headlock him.

Hip Into Him

Change your right arm from around his waist to around his right thigh and post your hand on your own thigh. From here, hip into him to keep him from getting on top of you. It is hard for you to gain control, but you can use this to drive him out of bounds.

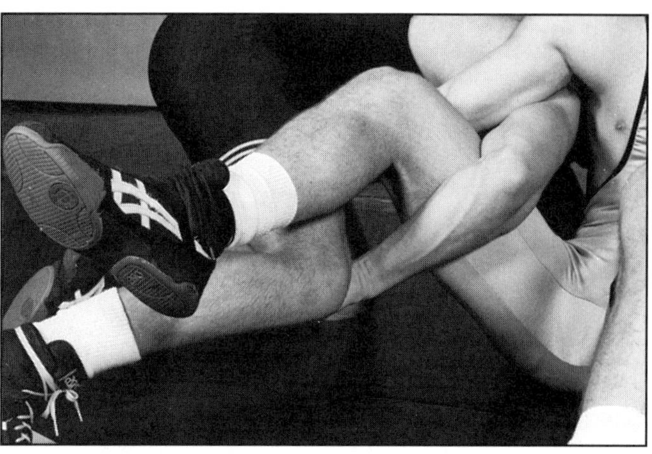

ROLLS

Each roll involves securing one of your opponent's arms to both pull him tight to your body and eliminate a post. The second common element gives the name to the move—you roll your opponent over you and ideally end up with a reversal. There are various rolls that can be initiated from the referee's position and there are situations rolls-specific rolls that can be done when the opponent is riding you a specific way.

Same-Side Roll

From the referee's position or any time that your opponent's arm is around your waist, grab his right wrist with your right hand and pull it tight across your waist. Roll to your right hip, keeping your head up, and elevate his left leg with your left leg by putting your instep underneath his ankle (a). As you are rolling, you can also use your left arm to help throw him over you (b). You can finish by releasing his wrist and turning toward his legs (he will most likely turn toward his base), and you will end up with a 2-point reversal. Or you can keep control of his right wrist as you scissors your left leg under your right leg and hold him on his back (c). For this roll and all other rolls, you need to have your head up. Never go down to your shoulder with your head on the mat because he could easily put in a half nelson (d).

a

b

c

d

Turn Inside

From the referee's position, step your inside knee back and drive your left elbow and head back toward your left knee. As you do so, reach between his legs and then around his right leg, putting you in the Peterson position. From here continue to turn back toward your feet and then roll him over, finishing with a Peterson (page 119, photo *c*, and page 125, *f* and *g*).

Cross-Wrist Roll

From either a referee's position or a tripod position, use your left hand to grab your opponent's right wrist (a). Post on your right hand and sit (whip) your hips under. Pull his arm across your waist and at the same time use your left leg to elevate his left leg if it is still there (usually it won't be) (b). You can finish with a headlock by reaching around his head with your right arm; a Peterson (page 119) by grabbing his right wrist with your right hand and reaching around his right leg with your left arm; or turn toward his legs and come into his crotch with a navy ride.

a

b

Sit-Out to a Roll

See the Sit-Outs section, page 125.

He Has a Cross Face Far-Ankle Ride

If the opponent has a cross face far-ankle ride on you, reach up with your left arm and control his left arm tight to your chest. Pull his arm down (if you can grab his forearm or wrist with your right hand, that helps), drive your left shoulder into him, post on your head (a), and then step your legs over to his other side (b and c). The harder he is picking up your ankle, the easier it is to step over him.

a

b

c

He Has Scooped Your Left Leg

He's got your left leg scooped? Three good options:

Sit-Back

If he hooks over your inside ankle with his right leg and is over your left arm (a), keep your left foot on the mat but rotate over it so that it is flat on the mat and traps his leg (b). At the same time, throw your left arm back under his arm, driving him back (c). He will end up on his back and you will have your leg on top of him and between his legs (d). Post your right leg behind you so he can't roll into you, reach under his right leg with your right arm, and with your left arm reach around his head. If his leg and head are close enough, you can cradle him with your leg still between his legs.

a

b

c

d

Trap His Left Ankle

If your opponent has your leg hooked as in the move just described (page 135, *a*), the following move can be done whether he is over or under your left arm: Lift your left foot up and pivot on your left knee, driving your hip into him, rotating your left foot over his left ankle (e). Control his right wrist with your right hand, post on your left arm, and continue to drive your hips into and then across the top of him (f). You need to get your hips completely over to his right side. You can adjust to end up in the same position as the last move or you can step your left leg out from between his legs and scissor it under your right leg (g).

Sit-Out

This is not a roll, but it's a good alternative when he has your left leg scooped. Step your right leg up and push back into him until your left foot is free (h). Then do a sit-out to get your leg free.

e

f

g

h

You Are on Your Knees and He Puts You in a Half Nelson

This is described on page 143 in the next chapter.

GRANBYS

This move was named after the school that developed and popularized it—Granby High School in Virginia.

Granby From Referee's Position

Post on your left arm, raise your hips, and grab your opponent's right wrist with your right hand (a). Tuck your head and look to your right, step your left leg underneath your right leg so he can't hook it with his right leg, and then push off your feet and drive over your shoulders (b). Roll across the top of your shoulders, not across your back. If he follows you, he usually is at least momentarily high or up by your head. If so, grab the inside of his right leg and finish with a Peterson (page 125). If he does not follow you, you should be able to roll all the way through for the escape or keep control of his wrist (c) and then spin around him for a reversal.

a

b

c

Granby From a Sit-Out

From a short sit, with your legs in close to your butt and planted so that you can drive off of them, control your opponent's right wrist with your right hand. It is easier if he is either grabbing your left arm or hooked over it rather than under it (a). For all Granbys it helps if he chops your left arm since this gives you momentum and drives his weight forward. Drop down to your left shoulder and roll across the top of your shoulders (b and c, next page). Finish as you did with the last Granby (*c*, above).

a

b

c

Granby From Standing

With your opponent behind you, you can do a Granby just as you did from the sit-out position. Push off your left foot, tuck your head, control his right arm around your waist, and finish as just described.

COUNTERS TO THE GRANBY

Hooking His Inside Leg

If you know your opponent is going to try to Granby, you can ride him with his near leg hooked (page 135, photo *a*). Without that leg free, he can't Granby.

Posting Your Hand

As the opponent rolls across his shoulders, post your right hand on the mat (a). As he completes his Granby you then spin behind him (b).

a

b

Roll With Him

If you are under both his arms, you can kick your legs over your opponent's as he Granby's. You should not try this if you are not under both arms since you will likely end up in the Peterson position (page 125).

4

Breakdowns, Rides, and Pins

Although we attempt to categorize different moves, many moves actually belong in more than one category. A *breakdown* is a move designed to break your opponent down to the mat, off of his base. A breakdown, though, may lead directly to a ride or a pin. Strictly speaking, a *ride* is a maneuver used to maintain control in the top position. Ideally, though, a ride will also break your opponent down and lead to a pin. A *pinning combination* is a move that directly turns your opponent to his back, possibly leading to a pin. In addition, a pinning combination such as an arm bar or a half nelson can be an excellent ride.

It is important to realize that as with takedowns, chain wrestling is extremely important. Many pinning opportunities arise just as a takedown is being completed or in the middle of a flurry of moves. To be a pinner, you must always be aware of the opportunities that arise.

The last point to emphasize about riding and pinning concerns *intensity*. Much more so than with the takedowns or escapes, successful riding requires great intensity and hard work. Many wrestlers who are poor riders have only laziness to blame. It is hard work to ride, but if you accept this and are willing to work hard you can become a good rider. The person who tries to hang on or to put legs in without setting them up because he is not willing to exert the extra effort will consistently get himself in trouble.

Decide right now to become a good rider so that if the situation arises where you have to be able to ride your opponent, you can. It is much better to make the commitment now than after you have lost in overtime because you could not ride your opponent for 30 seconds.

BREAKDOWNS AND RIDES

Jam and Rotary Breakdown

In this breakdown you first jam into your opponent and then rotate him down. On the whistle, drive off both feet and hit or jam under both of his arms and drive your chest into him (a). This will occasionally break some opponents down flat, but usually it will just stop their initial move, and that is what it is primarily designed to do. It is important that you are up on your toes and off your knees so that you can move easily. After you have jammed him and stopped his initial move, leave your left arm underneath his left arm, bring your right arm to the inside of his right thigh, and circle your feet toward his head. As you circle, if you pry up on his right leg and forward on his arm you should be able to break him down to his left side (b).

a

b

Knee Block

Start again by jamming into your opponent and under both arms, as shown in photo *a* in the previous section, but then bring both of your knees to either side of him. If you bring your knees to his left side, bring your right knee up far enough to block his left knee. Use your left hand to chop his left elbow, your right hand to pry on the inside of his right thigh, as shown, and pull him over your knee.

This move can also be tried if your opponent is stalling or just trying to keep a wide base to prevent you from breaking him down. If you are not able to pick his ankle or chop his arm effectively, using the thigh pry in addition to chopping his arm will usually help break him down.

Chop Near Arm

Chop your opponent's near (left) arm and at the same time jam into him with your chest while driving your right knee into his butt. You can use your right arm for a tight waist and break him down with this combination, or after you have chopped his left arm and brought it back to his waist, you can use your right hand to grab his left wrist. If both your knees are on his left side and you are chopping an arm, he could hit a Granby or a switch. By driving into him with your chest and bringing your knee into his butt, you make both of those moves much more difficult.

Head Lever

Slide your left hand down from your opponent's elbow to his wrist. This may be difficult to do as the initial move, but once you have stopped his initial move it can be done easily. Keep a tight waist or else pry on the inside of his right thigh with your right arm, and put your head in the back of his left armpit. You can either post his left hand down on the mat and drive his shoulder over his wrist, or as you drive into his armpit you can pull his wrist back to you. Break him down flat (a) and be up on your toes putting significant pressure on his arm. You can use the near wrist for a ride, but it is better if you can pop your head underneath his arm (b) and then change to a half nelson.

a

b

Cross Face Far-Ankle

You have a cross face any time your arm is across his face, usually turning it away. Use your left arm to cross face him so that you have turned his head to his right and are controlling his right arm above the elbow, as shown. At the same time, pick his outside ankle and then drive directly into him. Keep control of his far leg after you have broken him down.

"Ankle" Picks

Outside Ankle Pick

If you want to use this move, you may want to line up back toward your opponent's hips so that you are closer to his ankles. However, unless you always do an ankle pick or you always line up back toward his hips, this may give away your planned breakdown. On the whistle, pick his outside (right) foot at the laces (not the ankle) and change your left arm to around his waist. As soon as you pick his "ankle," pick it up to his butt, get up on your feet (a), and run him forward until he breaks down. Once he breaks down, trap his foot to his buttock and keep it there while you work for a pinning hold. (It is legal to hold his foot this way as long as the heel goes to the buttock and not the side of his hip.) If he moves his outside ankle before you can pick it, keep your right hand moving toward you and pick his inside ankle (b). Then, just as for the outside ankle pick, pick it up and drive him forward.

Inside Ankle Pick

Pick the laces of your opponent's inside shoe with your left hand. You need to scoot around behind him enough so that you can pick that ankle up, then drive him forward.

Knee Block Ankle Pick

Pick his far ankle with your right hand, reach your left arm over his head and hook his right shoulder, then chop his left knee with your left knee (a). Use your shoulder hook and your ankle control to pull him over your left knee and onto his side (b). If you can pinch or hook his left leg, you may be able to hold him long enough to get back points. Another option is to put your legs in on him, or you can simply scoot your hips up on top of him and go for another pinning combination.

a

b

c

d

Pump Handle With His Left Wrist

A *pump handle* is a ride and potential pinning hold that involves reaching in between your opponent's thighs and holding his wrist. With a little imagination it resembles grabbing a pump handle.

Stack

Begin by chopping your opponent's near arm and pulling it back to his waist. Reach between his legs with your right arm and grab his wrist (a). From here you can use your left hand to post on his head and lift his wrist to stack him (b). You can also come up to your feet, lift him off the mat, and drive him to his back.

Arm Bar

If your opponent goes flat to his stomach and puts his outside hip down, keep control of his left wrist with your right hand, get an arm bar on the near side (c), and run him over to his back using the arm bar.

Hip Tilt

If your opponent puts his inside hip down, use your left arm to hook his far arm (d), pull him on top of your left hip, and then hip tilt him (e). Use your right foot to lift under his left leg to help turn him.

a

b

c

d

e

Pump Handle With His Right Wrist

Another version of the pump handle is to control your opponent's right wrist with your right arm.

Hip Tilt

Once you have his wrist, hook his right arm with your left arm (a), and hip tilt him as described above.

Arm Trap

Walk around toward your opponent's head to bait him to grab your right leg (b). When he does, step your legs over his head. Keep his arm hooked with your leg and take him to his back (c). Finish with a reverse half nelson.

a

b

c

Half Nelson

Most wrestlers learn very early not to put the half nelson on when your opponent is on his knees since he could roll you. This is true if you are behind him (a). All he needs to do is trap your arm with his forearm, lower his shoulder to the mat, and then kick his legs over you (b). However, the half nelson can be used very effectively as a ride if you are positioned correctly. Your left shoulder needs to be above his shoulder, your legs need to be perpendicular rather than parallel to him, and your right arm should be prying on his far thigh (c). From here, circle toward his head to break him down flat.

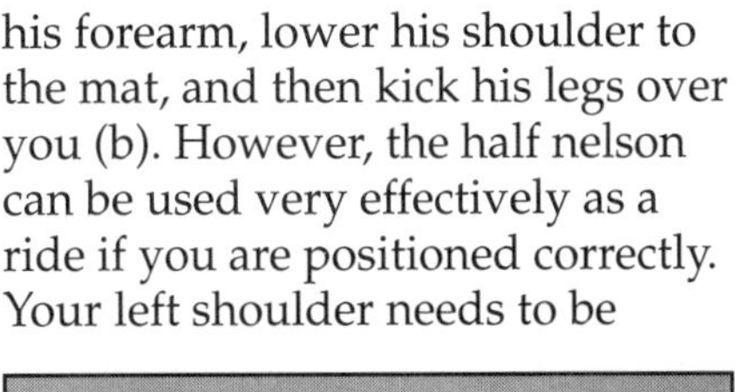

a

b

c

Finish by Pulling Him Underneath You

If you are circling your opponent and he is countering by pushing back into you, you can use his force to pull him toward you and to his back (d).

Finish by Controlling His Right Wrist

If he posts his right hand as a brace, change your right hand from his thigh to controlling his right wrist (e). Drive him over his wrist or pull his wrist underneath him, taking away his brace and making it easier to turn him over.

Finish With a Crotch Lift

You can also come into your opponent's crotch with your right arm, and then pick him up and turn him over (f).

Finish by Stacking Him

If you can get enough pressure down on his head with a half nelson, you can take your opponent straight over his head and stack him (g).

d

e

f

g

PINNING COMBINATIONS

Recall that a *pinning combination* is a move that turns your opponent on his back, possibly leading to a pin. There are a variety of pinning combinations, including the nelson series, arm bars, arm on his back, near-wrist control, cradles, and legs. As we said before, opportunites for pinning often arise just after a takedown or during a flurry of moves. The best wrestlers are opportunistic and are always ready to take advantage of a chance to put or catch an opponent on his back.

NELSON SERIES

The half nelson is probably the most common pinning hold, but few in wrestling know the origin of the name of the nelson series. It is from Lord Nelson, an 18th-century British naval hero, but the original meaning of the term was not sports-related at all. "Putting the Nelson on him" meant doing something devastating to someone.[1] In every move of the nelson series, one of your arms is under one of your opponent's arms and on top of his head. What differs with the different types of nelsons is where you are in rela-

[1]Thanks to Don Sayengo of Bethelem, Pennsylvania, and to the Wrestling Hall of Fame for this information.

tion to your opponent and where your other arm is. In a quarter nelson, you are in front of your opponent and the other arm is on his head (page 40). In a half nelson, you are off to his side and the other hand is not on his head (page 149, photo *d*). In a three-quarter nelson, you are off to the side and your other hand is under his chest and your hands are locked on top of his head (page 153, photo *a*). In a power half nelson, your other arm is underneath his other arm and locked up with your other hand (pp. 166–167). The full nelson, which is reaching under both of your opponent's arms from the back and having your hands on his head, was the main submission hold in early wrestling. This certainly meets the criteria of doing something devastating to an opponent. The full nelson is now illegal in scholastic wrestling.

Half Nelson

As mentioned earlier, you can use a half nelson to both ride and turn your opponent when he is on his knees, but it is easier to turn him if you have him broken down flat. Come underneath his left arm and put your left hand on top of his head. If he knows you are going to put in a half nelson, it is very difficult to overpower him and get into the position shown in the photo. The best time to catch it is when he is on his side and his arm and elbow are already alongside his head. He is not voluntarily going to do this; the opportunity frequently arises as you are completing a takedown or just as you've broken him down. You must always be ready.

FINISHING THE HALF NELSON

Turn Him By Prying on His Thigh

Keep your weight on your opponent's back so he doesn't raise up, and get out perpendicular to him. Reach underneath his left thigh and onto the back of his right thigh, as shown. Then, get up on your toes and drive your chest into him, cranking with both arms to turn him over. As you turn him, sink your half deeper so that it is as tight as possible around his head.

Turn Him by Grabbing His Other Arm

Instead of reaching between your opponent's legs with your right arm, reach underneath his chest, grab his right arm, and then pull it toward you as you turn him with your half.

Turk

You can use your right arm to lift your opponent's left leg and then step underneath it with your right leg and hook over his right thigh. You can then turn him over to his back, as shown.

Grapevine

A *grapevine* is a pinning combination in which you have your opponent on his back and have either one (single grapevine) or both (double grapevine) of his legs wrapped up with your legs. The name is derived from the similarity of the legs in this move to a grapevine entwined around a post. If you have him over to his back but you are unable to pin him, you can step your legs over his hips so he is straddled (see photo). Hook your feet around his legs for a double grapevine. From this position, arch your back and lift his head off the mat so that he cannot bridge; also, pry his legs out so he cannot post with them.

COUNTER TO A HALF NELSON

Turn Your Head Away

As soon as your opponent starts to put his arm underneath your arm and on top of your head, drive that elbow down to the mat and turn your head away. At the same time, reach up with your left hand to try to pull his hand off your head, as shown.

Bridge

If your opponent is on your right side and has you on your back with the half nelson, bridge up on your head so your shoulders are off the mat, and have your left hand tight to your chest and your elbow next to your side. From here, turn into him and drive your left hand between your chest and him. To create the space for this, turn just as you come off your bridge.

Counter to the Counter

As your opponent tries to turn into you, catch his left arm with your right arm, as shown, and then take him back to his back.

THREE-QUARTER NELSON

Hook your opponent's left leg with your right leg. Then reach for a half nelson with your left arm and reach underneath his chest with your right arm, locking your hands around his head (a). Then tuck his head down toward you, and walk his left knee up toward his head, stacking him on his shoulders (b).

a

b

ARM BARS

Just as a prisoner can be immobilized if he has a bar behind his lower back and both his arms wrapped around it, your arm can serve as a bar, locking one of your opponent's arms behind his back.

In the basic arm bar position, you are hooked over one of your opponent's arms with your same-side arm. You can put your palm flat on his back, but you get more pressure if you have your fist in his back, as shown in the photo. Ideally, you want to have his elbow behind his back rather than along his side because in the former position you will have much more power and pressure and, conversely, he will have less power. The key to getting into arm bars is to be aware of them all the time.

GETTING INTO ARM BARS

From an Arm Chop

Chop your opponent's near elbow with your same-side arm. Whether as an initial move or not, as you pull his arm back, hook it with your arm. Once you have him flattened out, you can then sink your arm in deeper and get his elbow behind his back.

Arm Chop to Wrist Control

Chop your opponent's left arm with your left hand and grab his left wrist with your right hand as you break him down. He will usually use his right hand to try to reach back and free his wrist. If he does, hook underneath it with your left elbow, keeping elbow pressure down on his back so that he cannot raise up (a). Then use your right arm to put in an arm bar (b).

a

b

He Pushes Up With His Elbows Out

Any time your opponent's elbows are out, you can put in an arm bar. If you have broken him down and he comes up to his base by doing a push-up with his elbows out (instead of coming up the right way, as described in the Basic Skills section (page 4), you can put in either a single or a double arm bar. You can force him to come up to a base the wrong way by pinching his knees together so that he can't bring a knee underneath him.

Head Lever

Grab your opponent's left wrist and drive your head into his armpit. After you have broken him down, bar him with your left arm.

Both Arms Locked Around His Arm

After you have broken your opponent down, lock both of your hands around your opponent's left arm (a). Have your chest down tight to his arm and then lift with your hips and back to raise his arm up. As you do, change your left arm to an arm bar (b). It may be possible to jerk his arm up enough by pulling with your arms and not your hips and back. However, since your hips and back are much stronger than your arms, it is more effective to use them.

a

b

Near Wrist Control

With near wrist control (one-on-one) on his left side, bring your left hip up under your opponent's arm to trap it, as shown. If his arm is trapped well, you can let go of it with your left arm and then use your left arm to apply an arm bar on the same side. Most of the time, how-ever, you will need to also grab him with your right hand as just described.

TURNS USING THE ARM BARS

Arm Bar to a Half Nelson

You first have to get your opponent's right arm tucked in to his body so that he cannot post with it. To do this, set your right elbow on the mat outside his arm and scoop it back to his side (a). Hold his arm there and drive your arm bar up toward his head and over his right shoulder. Keep your chest facing down to the mat and keep your weight directly over his shoulders (b). If your back is facing the mat, or if you get too high (too high means that the majority of your weight is centered above his head or behind him) (c), he could roll you through (d).

a

b

c

d

As you drive, keep walking toward his head. If he has his head turned away and is blocking with it, use your legs and your back to arch and get his left shoulder and head off the mat and then continue to drive him over. Once you have his weight posted on his right shoulder (b), you don't have to keep his arm tucked anymore. Instead, bring your right arm over to replace your bar (left) arm (e). Then use your left arm to put in a deep half nelson (f). Get chest to chest, and drive him over to his back.

e

f

Walk Around His Head

Keep the arm bar in, and walk all of the way around your opponent's head. Use your right arm to put in a reverse nelson.

Arm Bar/Underhook Walk Around His Head

Underhook his right arm (a), pull his arm tight to his side, and then walk around his head (b). He will likely try to kick over you. If he does, keep his arms tight and turn your right hip down into the mat to take him to his back.

a

b

Arm Bar/Underhook to Half Nelson

If your opponent counters the move just described by turning his head away and dropping his left shoulder, use the underhook on the far side to put in a half nelson (c). Either stay on his left side and stack him, or jump to his right side and drive him from there.

If he counters the half nelson by turning his right shoulder and hip down, this will turn his left shoulder and hip up, making it easier to turn him with the arm bar, as described above.

c

Hook the Legs In

Step across your opponent's back, keeping the arm bar in, and hooking your left heel on his left thigh as you go (see photo). Your right knee should be blocking his right hip. As you pull him toward his back, keep adjusting your hips on top of him so that you don't get them caught underneath him. Keep his left leg hooked with your leg and his left arm with your arm, and drive your elbow to his ear.

Post on His Head

Use your right arm to post on your opponent's right shoulder or head. If you can, grab your own wrist (a). Then, gradually shift your weight over the back of him (b). When you have him on his side, you can reach behind his head and hook his chin with your right hand or come over the front of his head and put in a half nelson.

a

b

Stack

If your opponent comes up on his knees, step your right knee in front of his left knee (a). Pry out on his right thigh and pull him over your knee to stack him (b).

a

b

Arm Bar/Wrist Control

If your opponent is flat on his stomach, and you are able to reach your right hand around his waist and grab his left wrist (a), either stack him by pulling down over your knee (b), or pull him onto your left hip and then hip tilt him.

a

b

ARM ON HIS BACK

While you could easily ride an opponent with this move as long as you wanted (or as long as the referee allowed), the more difficult parts of the move are getting into it and pinning people with it.

From an Arm Bar

From an arm bar, grab your opponent's wrist with your right hand (a) and twist his forearm so that his palm is facing up (this makes it difficult for him to free his arm) (b).

a

b

From Near-Wrist Control

From near-wrist control (see page 156) you may be able to drive your opponent over his arm or pull his arm underneath him and then up on his back. Frequently though, he will be pulling his arm underneath him and you won't be able to pull it out as just described. In that case grab his arm with both hands (as shown in photo *a* on page 148) and actually use your legs and back to help lift it up and onto his back.

FINISHES WITH HIS ARM ON HIS BACK

Trap His Arm on Your Thigh

If you are going from an arm bar to your opponent's arm on his back, as shown above, before completely removing your arm bar, lift his arm up and step your right leg across his back, as shown. Then settle your weight and take him to his back. You can leave your left arm in or remove it as you are taking him over to his back.

★ Reach Under His Far Arm

If he is flat on the mat, bend your opponent's elbow and control his hand on his back with your right hand (a). Then, circle around in front of him and with your left hand come underneath his right arm and grab his wrist (b). Change your right hand to a half nelson, get chest to chest and perpendicular to him, and drive him to his back, keeping control of his left wrist with your left hand. If he is keeping his head and right arm tight to each other preventing you from getting under his right arm, use your left elbow to pry his head toward you to create a space (c), then reach under his arm as just described. Another way of turning him is to hook his chin (d), lift his head and chest up (e), and turn him (f) while holding his left arm behind his back.

a

b

c

d

e

f

Hip Tilt

If your opponent is turning his left hip down, put your left forearm or elbow on his left arm (you can get a lot of pressure). Grab his right hip with your right hand and pull him up onto your left hip. Once here, you can hip tilt him. (The keys to the hip tilt are described on pp. 156–157.)

Hook His Far Arm

Use your right arm to underhook your opponent's right arm (a). From here block his left hip with your left knee and tilt him to his back. If he counters by turning his right hip down, roll him over to his right, pulling him into your right hip and changing your right underhook to a one-on-one as you go. Finish with a hip tilt to the other side (b).

If you can't hook and lift his right arm because he has shifted his weight to have his right hip down and his left hip up, step your left leg up and kneel on his left arm. If you get enough pressure, this will turn his left side down (and lift his right side), making it possible to hook his right arm (c). Finish the hip tilt as just described.

a

b

c

NEAR-WRIST CONTROL

Near-wrist control is simply controlling your opponent's wrist by being under his arm and over his wrist. If your hips are on one side of him, "near" makes sense. If your hips are straddling his, there is not really a near or far wrist. The term one-on-one implies you are controlling one of his arms with one of yours. It can be used both as a ride and to set up various pinning combinations.

The Near Wrist

If your opponent is lying flat with his arms out in front of him, reach underneath his left arm and grab his left wrist (a). If possible, simply pull it back underneath him. Usually you won't be able to do this; it is more effective to use your legs to drive his body over his wrist (b).

a

b

Finishes With the Near Wrist

Half Nelson

If your opponent posts up on his right arm (a), the half nelson is open. You will most likely need to jump over to that side to drive it, since otherwise he will turn his right hip down and be able to get his arm down and you will not have any power.

★Hip Tilt

In this move you tilt or turn your opponent's shoulders by tilting his hip. With your right arm, grab his right thigh and lift him onto your left hip (b). At the same time slide your right foot under his left leg. If you are having problems getting his hip up on yours, you may need to reach between his legs and grab his left thigh and then lift from there. Tilt him toward his back, pulling with your right hand on his hip and lifting with your right leg under his leg (c). If you are having problems tilting him enough to get any back points, use your right leg to lift his left leg even higher. You probably won't pin anyone with this move, but you should be able to hold your opponent for a minimum of 2 and usually 3 back points. Make sure his thigh is on your hip, tight in your lap. If he is not on top of your hip, it is difficult to turn him at all. If there is space between your hips and his, it will be harder to hold him on his back and he will have a better chance of turning into you and getting a reversal. Keep control of his left arm throughout the move. Your left arm control may be enough to keep him from being able to turn into you. However, if he does kick hard and starts to get his hips over you, slip your right hand from his right hip into a Navy ride (over his right hip and under his left hip) and scissors your left leg under your right to get your hips out.

a

b

c

Arm Pry

If your opponent counters the hip tilt by turning his left hip up, shifting his weight to his right hip so that you can't tilt him, pull his near wrist out from under him and walk around toward his head so that your knees are straddling his head. Your left knee will be just to the outside of his head and your right foot will be planted so that you can drive off of it. As you walk toward his head, you have to keep weight and pressure on his right shoulder with your left elbow so that he can't raise up. Once you have his head blocked, use both of your arms to pull his arm directly toward you (d), not straight across his back. When his arm is up high enough, slip your right arm between his arm and his side (e), and put in a half nelson with your left arm. Get chest to chest and drive him over. If you are doing this move in freestyle, you can jerk his arm and allow him to roll through across his shoulders to get tilt points.

Hip Tilt From Referee's Position

Although this is not a near wrist variation, it is a variation of the hip tilt and it is best explained here. On the whistle, chop your opponent's near arm and use your tight waist to pull him onto your hip. Place your right foot underneath his left leg and tilt him as just described. You won't have quite as much control of his left arm, but it should certainly be enough to tilt him.

d

e

CRADLES

When a small child is cradled in someone's arms, one arm needs to be around the child's neck and the other arm behind his knees. The cradles described here are similar in that the final position involves holding your opponent on his back with one arm under a knee and the other one around his head. There are several types of cradles that have different set-ups and involve locking around your opponent's legs in different ways.

Far-Side Cradle

If your opponent attempts to stand up and comes up on his right (or far) foot, bringing his knee up toward his head, drive your left arm over his left shoulder and around his chest and your right arm over his back and around his knee (a). Lock your hands either with your fingers or palm-to-palm as with a single leg. Step both of your legs over to his right side and then drive into him to get him down to his left hip (b). Step your right leg underneath his right leg and drive it forward (c). Walk toward his head until he is on his side, ready to go over to his back. Then, step across him with your left leg first so that your hips remain facing down to the mat. Once you have him over, drive your left knee into his side, pull the side of his head into your head, and use your right leg either to post behind you so that he can't turn into you (d), or scissors his left leg. If your left shoulder is underneath his shoulder, this will prevent you from getting the pin. If that is the case, you need to scoot your hips and your shoulder out from underneath him.

a

b

c

d

★ If He Gets His Arm Out

If you have the far-side cradle locked up and step over your opponent's right side, but then he gets his right arm out (e), as soon as he gets it out, keep your hands locked and jump back across his back, taking him to his back (f).

Alternate Finish to the Far-Side Cradle

As you reach over to lock up the cradle, you can keep your momentum going and in the same motion essentially dive over your opponent (g), tucking your head underneath him and pulling him across you (h). Finish as shown in photo *d.*

e

f

g

h

Cross Face Cradle

If Your Opponent Is Flat on the Mat

Cross face your opponent and control his right arm above his elbow, keeping his head turned. Post your right arm between his legs and then run around toward his head, driving his head and arms to his right knee (a). Don't try to bring his leg up to his head with just the power of your right arm because you won't be able to do it. Keep holding his right arm with your left hand and lock your right hand onto your wrist. Pull him back, allowing his right shoulder to slide off yours and down to the mat. Finish as with the far-side cradle, just described.

a

If He Is Up On a Good Base

Cross face your opponent and grab his right arm. Grab his right ankle (b) and pick it up as you pull his arm toward you, which should set him on his butt. Release his ankle and put your hand underneath his right leg. Then, drive his head down to his foot, grab your wrist, hold his right arm, and take him back to his back.

b

Near-Side Cradle

You can get into the near-side cradle if your opponent does a poor inside-leg stand-up, keeping his head down so that his head and knee are close to each other (a). Or, if he is lying flat on the mat, put your left arm around his neck, your right arm around his left leg, your head in his side, and drive into him so that he doubles up and you can lock your hands (b).

To Finish, Stack Him or Hook His Left Leg

If you can get your opponent's right shoulder tucked in (by crunching him up), you can drive him directly onto his shoulders. Once you have him on his back, finish by hooking his left leg with your right foot and planting it on the mat (c).

To Finish, Scoop His Left Leg

Walk back toward your opponent's legs and scoop his top (left) leg first with your right leg (d) and then with your left leg to get his leg trapped on your left thigh. Walk up toward his head, stacking him (e) as in the previous move.

a

b

c

d

e

Cradle When He Is Off His Knees

Sit Underneath Him

If you cannot get your opponent down to his knees (a) or take him over with any of the other moves just described, sit your left leg underneath him, tucking his head and rolling his butt over his head (b). Roll over to your back, pulling him over you onto his back (c). You can try to hold him like that but be careful—you could pin yourself. Or, you can post on your head and get on top of him (d).

a

b

c

d

Roll Underneath Him

Rather than taking your opponent's leg and butt over his head as in the previous move, this move pulls his leg under his head. Use your right arm to crunch his left knee underneath him, then roll across your back (e and f). As with the previous move, it is best to step your right leg over and finish on top of him.

As you pull his left leg forward make sure that your left leg is back so that he does not catch his left foot underneath it and elevate you over to your back (g).

e

f

g

★ Leg Cradles

Scoop your opponent's right ankle with your right foot while placing your left forearm across his head and reaching under his right arm with your right arm and locking your hands. Pry up on his shoulder and down on his head, driving his head down to the mat (a). If you let him keep his head up, he can drive back into you, reversing you (page 135). Once his head is planted on the mat, walk his left knee up to his head (b). When his head and knee are close enough, step your left knee up to block his left shoulder (c). Pinch your knees together, reach into his crotch, and pull him over your left knee, stacking him.

a

b

c

COUNTERS TO CRADLES

The first and best counter is to be aware of the positions that your opponent could possibly cradle you in and avoid them.

His Hands Are Locked but You Are on Your Base

If your opponent does get a cradle locked up, try to break his grip immediately, using your hands to attack his hands and driving your leg back. If you can't break his grip, turn your inside hip down, as shown, making it more difficult for him to take you to your back.

You Are on Your Back

If your opponent does get you over to your back, this is definitely the time to fight with all the fury you can. If he has you stacked up, you want to keep rocking back and forth so that your shoulders are never on the mat long enough to be pinned. As you are rocking, attack his grip with your hands and try to explode your left leg away from him to break his grip. You can get more power by hooking your left leg with your right leg so that you can use the power of your hips to break his grip.

LEGS

"Legs" is the general term used to describe a ride and a series of pinning combinations in which the key control is from one of your legs hooking one of your opponent's.

■ *When opponent is on his base,* your left heel should be hooked just inside of his left thigh (a) and your right foot can be planted between his legs so that your right thigh and knee are driving forward on his butt. Your hips should be in back of his hips, not on top of him. This gives you more power. As an alternative with your right foot, you can lace it underneath his right foot and then use this foot to pry out on his leg and rotate him down to the mat.

You should *not* lace your left foot over your opponent's left leg because this places your knee underneath him (see photo *a* on page 177), taking away a post and making it quite easy for him to turn his inside hip down and get on top of you (see photo *b* on page 177). If only your heel is hooked, your knee can be out from between his legs, and if he tries to hip into you, your left knee will be acting as a brace.

■ *When he is broken down,* keep your weight on top of him, maximizing the pressure. You do not want to be laying diagonally across him with your chest and most of your weight off of him. You can either figure four his left thigh (b) above his knee, or plant your right knee just to the outside of his right knee, pinching it in so that he cannot get it out as a brace. The Figure Four is a way of controlling an opponent's leg when one of your legs is bent at the knee and wrapped around his leg, and the foot of that leg is hooked over your other leg, forming the number 4. This is legal if done around one of your opponent's legs, but it is not legal if done around the body or both his legs.

a

b

Various ways to get into Legs include the following six options.

Jam Breakdown

From the referee's position, jam under your opponent's arms to block them and to get his weight forward on them. Then, while still blocking his left arm, hook your left heel in, as shown.

Shoulder Hook/Ankle Pick

Use your left arm to hook your opponent's right shoulder and with your right hand grab his right ankle. Have your left knee just in front of his left thigh. Pick up his ankle and shoulder, and use your right foot to drive into him to get his weight forward and then hook your leg in. Or, you can pull his right shoulder and right ankle toward you, essentially pulling him onto your lap, as shown, and then put the legs in.

Pull Him Over His Right Ankle

Step your right foot to the outside of your opponent's right ankle, hook his left shoulder with your left arm, and force your left hip into him, driving him over to his side (see photo). Hook your legs in as you go. If done from the referee's position, this works better starting with the optional starting position with your hands on his back.

Pull Him on Top of You

One other way of getting into the legs when your opponent is in his base, and probably the laziest and least safe for you, is to hook under both of his shoulders and pull him back on top of you, putting in legs as you go. Instead of having him broken down, you end up on your butt, underneath him.

If He Counters the Hip Tilt

If you have a near-wrist control and your opponent is defending the hip tilt (photos *b* & *c* on page 157) by turning his right hip down, you should already have your left hip under his left hip, and therefore you can easily hook your legs in and then come up on top of him.

Lift His Leg

Alternatively, when your opponent is flat you can straddle his left leg with your legs, reach behind yourself, and first grab and then lift his left ankle (page 168, photo *a*). Then, hook the legs in. Keep pressure on his shoulders with your left forearm.

BREAKDOWNS WITH LEGS

Pry Out on His Right Leg

With your right foot in his instep (a), arch your hips into your opponent and pry out on his right foot (b). This should rotate him down flat.

Ankle Pick

You can pick up your opponent's right ankle with your right hand and drive into him.

He Is Coming Up to His Base

If you have your opponent broke down flat with your left heel hooked in on his left thigh and he starts to get his right knee underneath him to come to his base, hook under his right instep and pry out, similar to photo *a*. Alternatively, place your right foot on the front of his right thigh and push it back down to the mat.

a

b

PINNING COMBINATIONS USING LEGS

★Power Half When He Is on His Base

In this move your right arm is under your opponent's right arm as in a half nelson, but your left forearm is used on his head to increase your power. Bring your right foot up so that you are pinching his hips with your knees. Put your left forearm across the back of his head and reach under his right arm with your right arm and lock your hands (a). The deeper you can sink your right arm, the better. Turn your left elbow down toward the mat to turn his head down and away, and at the same time lift his right shoulder with your right arm. Drive him down to his side and then release your left arm and post up on it (b). This allows you to bring your hips up on top of him and sink your right arm even deeper. Turn the little finger side of your wrist against his head, not the palm of your hand as in a half nelson. If your palm is flat on his head, you do not have as much power in your wrist, and it is more difficult to keep him from getting his elbow back to his side. When you have him turned enough, release your legs and jump over to his right side and drive a half nelson. Alternatively, you could keep your legs hooked but you would have to rotate your hips on top of him.

a

b

Power Half When He Is Flat on the Mat

If you do the power half when your opponent is flat on the mat, the key step is still to turn your opponent's head away with your left forearm. Your left elbow should be on the mat, next to his head. The rest of the move is the same as just described.

Power Half When You Can't Reach Under His Right Arm

If your opponent is flat and has his right arm out in front of him and next to his head so that you can't reach under his shoulder, reach across with your left arm to grab his wrist. Lift his arm off the mat and then reach underneath his elbow with your right arm and grab your own wrist (a). Then, adjust your left forearm across his head and complete the move as described above.

Counter to the Power Half. If your opponent is working for a power half, throw your left shoulder down and your right shoulder and arm up (b), causing him to slide off of the top of you. If you wait until he has tucked your chin down to your chest the move will likely not work.

a

b

Back Breaker

Scoop your opponent's left leg with your right heel so that you can reach back and pick up his right foot. After you pick his heel up, hook your right heel as high up on his thigh as possible (a). Hold his foot as you cross face him with your left arm and try to drive his head and heel together (b). If needed, you can get additional power by hooking your left heel on his left thigh, then arch him over.

a

b

Cross Face

If your opponent has his arms out as posts, preventing you from turning him, as just described, cross face him and grab his upper right arm (see photo). Have the bony part of your forearm across his face so you can get more pressure. Use your legs to drive over him as you pull his right arm under him. Once flat, arch and turn him, as in photo *b*, above.

Crucifix or Guillotine

This move is a means of pinning, or "killing," your opponent when his arms end up at right angles to his body, as in a crucifix, or when secured in a guillotine.

Once you have your opponent broken down, grab his right arm with both hands and twist his wrist so that his palm is facing up. This locks his elbow so he can't bend it easily (a). Then, lift his arm up, turning him toward his back. Once you have him turned so that he is about half-way over, put his arm behind your head and reach your left arm behind his head (b). Do not place his arm behind your head if you don't have him at least half-way over because he will still be powerful enough to lock around your head and either reverse you or hold you for a stalemate. Once you have him to his back, lock your hands around his head and pull his head toward you (c). You can try this same move without having him broken down, but it is more difficult.

Countered Guillotine to a Hip Tilt

If you do try to hook underneath your opponent's right arm for a Guillotine while he is still up in his base and he pulls his arm down, reach between his legs with your right arm and grab his right wrist (d). Pull him up on your lap as you roll to your back, taking him to his back at the same time (e).

If He Counters the Hip Tilt

If you have reached between his legs and grabbed his right wrist and then he turns his right hip down, making it difficult for you to hip tilt him, put your head on the mat, unhook your legs (f) and walk your feet around toward his head, pulling him on top of your hips (g).

a

b

c

d

e

f

g

Spread Eagle

This is a potentially punishing pinning hold in which your opponent's thighs can be spread far apart, like the wings of an eagle. Lock your hands around his right thigh. Lift up and out on his knee, so that you are splitting him, and at the same time turn your left hip down into him (a). Arch your right foot back to get additional pressure. When you get enough pressure or pain, he will go over to his back. When he does, you can use your right leg to push his left leg even further away or you can post it behind you and drive into him to stack him up on his shoulders even more (b).

a

b

Back Arch

Bring your right knee up to block above your opponent's right hip (a). Put your feet together so that he cannot kick out. Have your weight directly over him and arch your back, lifting his left thigh and turning his hips toward the mat (b). Your right knee has to be tight to his right hip to turn him. In many cases you can turn him just with your hip pressure, but you can also hook his left shoulder to help pull him over. Just as he is ready to turn over to his back, you no longer need to block his hip with your right knee, so shift it away from him so that his hips don't roll on top of that knee.

a

b

Keep your left knee tight on his thigh, post on your right arm, and either cross face him (c) or hook his left shoulder with your left arm. If you hook his shoulder, drive your elbow to his ear. If he turns away, hook your left arm tighter and pull his left shoulder back to the mat. If he turns into you, step your left leg over his right leg and hook up the double grapevine (see page 146).

c

Legs and a One-on-One to a Hip Tilt

Get a one-on-one on your opponent's right side. If he is not in the position for you to get a one-on-one easily, use your right forearm to bring his right arm into his side, then grab his right wrist with your left hand. Then get a one-on-one with your right hand (a). From here, hip tilt him by blocking his right hip with your right knee, hooking your left foot under his right leg, and pulling him on top of you (by using your left leg hook and by hooking his left shoulder with your left arm) (b and c).

a

b

c

Hip Tilt to the Other Side

If you get to the position shown in photo *b* and can't tilt your opponent back because he is turning to his stomach, reverse your efforts and roll with him to his stomach and then to a hip tilt on the other side. As you roll, change your left arm from hooking under his left arm to a one-on-one (d) and change your right one-on-one to a right shoulder hook (e). Keep your hips tight to him throughout the move, and pull him onto your hips and over to his back.

Navy Ride

Another alternative if you can't turn your opponent from the position in photo *b* is to reach your left arm under his right leg (a navy ride) (f). Keep your one-on-one, and tilt him to his back (g).

d

e

f

g

★ Legs and Arm Bar to a Hip Tilt

If you have your left leg in and he is flat with both arms out as braces, preventing you from turning him with a back arch as described above (pp. 170–171), use your left arm to turn his head away. This shifts his weight to the left and allows you to put in an arm bar on the right (a). Keep his head down with your left hand and roll back over to his left side (b). Once his weight is shifted to his left hip, reach your left arm around his waist and grab his right wrist. (The move can be done without grabbing his wrist, but this step does make it much tighter.) Hook your right foot under his left leg and elevate him over to his back (c).

After you have held your opponent for your 3 back points, let him turn back to his base. As he does so, keep your hips tight to him and your left leg hooked, and roll on top of him. Release his wrist with your left arm and change to a cross face (d). Release your right arm bar but keep his arm to his side until he is up on his right side. "Picture frame" his head as you take him to his back (e).

a
b
c
d
e

Double Cross Face

Your opponent is flat on the mat and you are on top of him with his hips straddled or your left leg hooked in. Use your right hand to cross face him and get his head turned to the left (a). Reach your left arm so that your elbow is at his chin and your forearm is along the right side of his head keeping his head turned to the left (b). Lock his right thigh with your right knee and tilt him over to his back, hooking your left leg in as you do so (c).

a

b

c

Wrong Leg Hooked In

If you get your right leg hooked between your opponent's legs (a) (you most frequently get into this position by countering certain takedown attempts), you can drive a half nelson on the far side. First put on a power half as described before (see pp. 166–167), then sink your right arm (b). Alternatively, you can lock your hands around his right leg and spread eagle him (c).

a

b

c

COUNTERS TO LEGS BEFORE HE GETS THE LEGS IN

In any aspect of wrestling it is always better to make your opponent adjust to your style rather than vice versa. However, if he has consistently stopped your initial move and gotten legs in, you can consider one of the following as an initial move:

Solid Base

On the whistle, bring both of your elbows back to your thighs (to block him putting legs in) and shift your weight back to your feet. If your opponent tries to put legs in, he will have to be going over one of your arms (a) and you should be able to throw his leg behind you (b) to get out.

Simply forcing him to go over your left arm doesn't automatically stop him. If you wait too long to escape and he gets his leg hooked in, your arm will be trapped and he will have excellent control.

Short Sit-Out or Sit-Back

A short sit-out with hand control (see photos *a* & *b* on pp. 123–124) stops most of your opponent's options for getting legs in. Once you are in the sit-out position, he can possibly pull you back on top of him or turn you to your side and get legs in as he comes on top of you. With each of these moves, though, if you have hand control and are aware of his legs coming in, you should be able to stop him.

Catch His Leg

Regardless of what initial move you use, if you can catch your opponent's left knee or ankle (c) as he is trying to put legs in, throw that leg behind your back (b) and turn quickly to face him.

Inside Sit

This move, as described previously (see page 126), works well if your opponent is trying to jam into you to put the legs in.

a

b

c

COUNTERS AFTER HE HAS THE LEGS IN

Mule Kick

This works best just as your opponent is putting the leg in. Kick your left leg straight back and into the air, as shown. Once your leg is free, bring your knee back next to your other knee so he can't put the legs in again.

Grab His Ankle

One way of getting your opponent's right ankle is to sit back toward his feet (a). Or, if his left leg is hooked in deeply, you can bring his foot close to you by driving your left hip into him, forcing him to step his right leg behind him to keep from going down to his hip. When he does, grab his ankle.

Finishes Once You Have His Ankle

Drive into your opponent to knock him on his right hip (b). Just as you hit is the best time to scoot your hips away from him and try to gain control (it is a scramble position). You can also lift his right ankle, shifting his weight off of you, and then coming up on top with legs in yourself (c). As you are coming out from underneath him, you must get your hips away from him.

a

b

c

Forward Somersault

Come up off your knees (a) and then do a forward somersault (b). As you finish the somersault, slide your hips away from your opponent and reach for a headlock (c). His leg may still be hooked, so you have to make sure that your hips are not on top of his hips or he will probably be able to maintain control.

a

b

c

Drive Hip Underneath You

If your opponent makes the mistake of hooking his leg in deeply (a), turn your left hip down to the mat, driving him to his hip (b). Post your left hand on the mat and drive into his chest, forcing him to his back, and reach to block his left leg as you step your hips across him (c).

a

b

c

Step your left leg out from between his legs and then scissors your legs and reach for a reverse half nelson (d). Or, you can leave your left leg over his right leg and hook up a cradle (e). Whichever way you finish, you are still in a scramble position.

d

e

COUNTERS WHEN YOU ARE SITTING BETWEEN HIS LEGS

If you can drive your opponent over on his butt, he is going to be trying to come underneath your arms and hold your hips back tight into his lap. If he gets the chance, he will also try to cross face you (see photo) and take you back over to your stomach where he has more control. To get out of this position, you have the following options:

Fight for Hand Control

You don't want your opponent to be underhooked since he can hold you in his lap. First, work to get one side free and then hold that elbow in and work on the other side. Do not make the mistake of freeing one side and then as you work on the other side lifting the elbow up and letting him underhook that side again.

Slide Your Hips Down

This is best if you have already cleared at least one of your opponent's underhooks. Once you have, try to scoot your hips down toward his feet so that your hips are no longer on top of his. If you can reach under his leg, pull it up toward your head as you scoot your hips down. Try to put his leg behind your head as you slide your hips down and then turn into him (a and b).

a

b

Post on His Foot and Step Your Hips Out

If your opponent has your left leg hooked, put your right foot on top of his right ankle (a), post on your right hand, and slide your hips over to his right side (b). By posting on his ankle, he will not be able to scoot with you to keep you between his hips. Use your left hand to control his left foot.

a

b

Backward Somersault

Do a backward somersault straight back over your opponent's head and try to grab his head as you are going over (see photo). If his legs do not come unhooked but you have his head, you may be able to stack him.

Shin Pressure

Grab across the top of your opponent's feet, controlling the outside of his feet and twisting them in. At the same time, drive the bony part of your forearms into his shins, as shown. This puts a tremendous amount of pressure on the bony part of his legs, which can be quite painful. At the same time, slide your hips down and away from him and then turn into him.

5

Freestyle Turns

Freestyle and Greco-Roman wrestling are the wrestling styles in international competition, including the Olympics. The major difference between these styles and scholastic wrestling is the scoring. In freestyle and Greco-Roman, the emphasis is on turning your opponent to his back. He does not need to be held on his back any length of time to score—you only need to turn him so that his back is past 90 degrees and facing the mat. If you gain control with a takedown, you have only a limited time to try to get back points and then you both start in the neutral position again. There are no points for escapes.

Greco-Roman wrestling differs from freestyle wrestling in that you can't use your legs to hook or trip your opponent, nor can you attack your opponent's legs—only moves above the waist are allowed.

Some moves described here are illegal in scholastic wrestling. Others are listed because they result in your opponent just rolling across his shoulders and getting free, which would be worth 2 points for you in freestyle but would give your opponent 1 point in scholastic wrestling and none for you. However, except for the illegal moves, all of the following can either be used as described or with a slight modification to work in scholastic wrestling. In addition, it should be emphasized that these are not the only turns that can be used in freestyle—all of the pinning combinations previously described can, and should, be used in freestyle.

FREESTYLE TURNS AS COUNTERS TO TAKEDOWNS

★ Counter to the Head-to-the-Inside-Single

Block your opponent's right shoulder and head with your left knee, and with your right hand grab his left hip (a). Do not reach around his waist because he could roll you (pp. 25–26). You can then pull and lift his left hip over your knee, tilting his shoulders to the mat (b). Post on your left hand as you do this and stay up on top of him as much as possible rather than going down flat to your left side.

a

b

Then finish in one of the following three ways:

Finish by Letting Him Return to His Base

Once you have exposed your opponent's back, you can let him get back to his base. If he doesn't make any adjustments you can do the same move again.

Finish With a Reverse Half Nelson

As you take your opponent to his back, kick your right leg back hard to break his grip, then put in a reverse half nelson and adjust your weight to take him to his back (c).

Finish by Grabbing His Arm

If you can't break your opponent's grip and free your leg, use your right arm to hook under his right arm and then walk your leg back. If he holds on, he will go to his back (d).

c

d

Counters to the Head-to-the-Outside Single

Squat so that your right thigh is under your opponent's chest. Block his right arm with your left arm so he can't change to a double. As he comes up off his knees (a) post back on your right arm, reach around his waist with your left arm and roll him to his back (b). You can roll him through or hold him on his back by pinching his right arm with your thighs (c) and then putting in a reverse half nelson.

You can also "fall off" his right shoulder, blocking his right arm with your left knee and grabbing his right ankle. Then roll him to his back, pulling him over you and tilting him (d and e). Finish as shown in photo *c*.

a

b

c

d

e

Counter to a Low Single

Beside the counters previously discussed (pp. 42–45), if your opponent is in on a low single leg and is behind you (page 44, page bottom), you can pretend to "bail-out" by dropping down to your hands and knees as if conceding the takedown. Just as he reaches around your left leg to gain control (a), kick your left leg over him (b and c), exposing his back. If he already has your left ankle and the only thing keeping him from getting control is you driving back into him and holding his head down, you can do the same move by diving forward and kicking your left leg over his back at the same time.

a

b

c

FREESTYLE TURNS FROM DOWN ON THE MAT

There is no period that starts with both wrestlers down on the mat, but if you were in the process of turning your opponent as you went out of bounds or if he is called for stalling, you will start down on the mat (par terre position) and get the opportunity to turn him. If you have the top starting position, your thumbs must be together somewhere on his back. Your legs cannot be touching him but can be as close as you want. It is much easier to turn him if you can get him onto your hips. One way to help you do this is to have your left hip and knees bent forward so that your knee is in front of his left thigh. Then, if he's trying to flatten out on the whistle, you can drive your thigh underneath him so that he ends up on top of your hips.

On the bottom, you can either try to stay up on your hands and knees in a good base and fight for hand control as he tries various turns, or you can flatten out. If you choose to flatten out, instead of just going flat, it is more effective to turn into your opponent, driving your same side (left) hip up and your elbow back into his side, as shown. This makes it much more difficult for him to get his hips under yours as just described.

There are no points for an escape but the most effective way to counter his turns is to get away. You can get away by simply crawling forward as fast as you can since unlike in scholastic wrestling, he will be expecting you to stay still and will be more concerned with applying a hold to turn you with than one to keep you from getting away.

★ Crotch Lift

To do this move, you need to have your arms locked around your opponent's right thigh and your left hip under his left thigh (a). From this position, get off your butt and arch straight back toward his head (b). Don't break his back, but bend him enough so that he wants to turn. Slightly ease off on your back pressure for a moment to get him to relax, then throw him over his left shoulder (c). You can try to do this slowly and stack him, or you can roll him all the way through. If you do the latter, you need to come up to your base quickly to face him in case he tries to come back into you.

You can turn your opponent easier if you pull his right ankle up to his butt and lock around it and his thigh. Similarly, if you can pull his right heel up to his butt, hold it there with your chest, and adjust your arms so that you are around his left thigh but still have his right foot trapped (d), the turn is even easier.

a

b

c

d

Counter to the Crotch Lift

Get up on your hands, turn your right hip down to the mat, look back toward him, and put your left elbow into his side (e).

Counter to the Counter—the Turk

Unlock your arms, use your right arm to lift your opponent's left thigh, and step into a turk (f). Then, drive him over to his back. Hook your legs in. If he has his right hip down and his left hip up, it should be easy to slide your left leg under his left leg to hook up the legs.

e

f

★ Gut Wrench

This move can be done with your arms locked only around your opponent's waist (or gut), but is more effective if you can also trap one of his arms to his side so that he won't have a brace on that side (a). Because you are locking your hand around his body, it is illegal in scholastic wrestling.

Once you are in this position, you head should be flat on your opponent's back facing away from the direction you are going to turn him. Keep his back tight to your chest, step your right leg over your left leg, bridge up into him, and throw your hips into him (b and c). As long as you bridge, you won't give away any back points. If you stay locked up, you can repeat this move as much as you want and score each time.

a

b

c

Counter to the Gut Wrench

You can crawl forward a few inches keeping your stomach tight to the mat, which turns your opponent's hands under you, taking away his power. You can also try turning back into him as described for the counter to-the-crotch lift.

High Gut Wrench

Rather than being around your opponent's waist, you can have your hands locked around his chest (a). Keep your chest tight to his back and pull him up on your left hip. Then do a hip tilt to the left side (b). Or, fake tilting him to the right side, getting him to react to the left, and then tilt him to the left. You can hold him there to try to get three points, or you can roll him through. Once locked around his chest, you can also come up to your feet and then roll onto your back. The key is keeping your chest tight to his back!

a

b

★ Leg Wrench

If your opponent is already flat on the mat or as he is going flat, lock both your arms around his thighs as tightly as you can (a). Lift his thighs into your chest and drive your shoulders into his butt or lower back to get his chest flat on the mat. You can take him either way, but turn your head away from the side you're going to take him. If taking him to the left, step your right leg over your left leg, then bridge into him, keeping his thighs tight to your chest (b). As with the gut wrench, you can do this move continuously and score 2 points each time. Also, you can fake to one side and as he reacts, turn him to the other side.

a

b

If you can't turn your opponent because his left arm is out as a post, control his thighs just above his knees with your right arm. Use your left arm to chop his left arm and use your left knee to block his left hip (c), then tilt him.

c

★ Ankle Cross

This is a series of moves in which the power for turning your opponent comes from crossing (twisting) his legs. To get into an ankle cross from an ankle pick, start by picking up your opponent's right ankle toward his butt. If he is keep his knee stiff, preventing you from bending his knee and picking up his ankle, try picking up his left ankle first. He will usually resist you vigorously on that leg, but if you let it go you will be able to pick up the right ankle quickly because it will be relaxed. Once you have the ankle up, cover it with your chest and then drop down to his left ankle and wrap your arm around it (a).

a

Finish with the Standard Leg Cross Turn

Use your left arm on your opponent's butt or lower back to keep him flat on his belly (b).

b

c

d

Come up to your feet while keeping downward pressure on him. Drive his feet straight over his back to flatten him (c), and then use your right hand to twist his legs and drive him over to his shoulders (d). You can roll him through and let him go; try to stack him by dropping his knees toward his head; or let him return to his chest, retighten your arm control, and repeat the same move.

Counter to the Ankle Cross—Block Him From Locking It Up

As soon as your opponent pulls your right ankle up to your butt, step your inside (left) knee up so you come to your base and shift your weight back on your feet.

Counter to the Ankle Cross—Walk on Your Hands

Come up and walk on your hands, looking back into him so that he can't get the proper angle to turn you.

Counter to Walking on the Hands

If you are doing the ankle cross, and your opponent counters as just described, walk backward to get your opponent off his hands and back onto his chest, then proceed to turn him as described previously.

Counter to the Ankle Cross—Grab His Ankle

Use your right hand to grab your opponent's left leg or ankle (e). Block his ankle and drive into him to take him down to his butt, possibly getting back points (f).

e

f

Leg Lock

If your opponent is on his hands and knees in a good base, get to his left side, reach your left arm in front of his left thigh, and grab his right leg just below the knee. With your right arm, grab his right ankle (a). Then, drive your left shoulder into his hip and pull his outside leg to you, driving him over to expose his back (b). To pin him, keep his knees locked together and pull them tight to your chest. Turn your left hip down and arch your back to the mat. This lifts his legs still more and stacks his shoulders on the mat (c).

a

b

c

Step Over His Head

Pick up his inside thigh and put it on your hip. Step your left leg over his head (a) and in the same motion lift his left thigh up and drive over your left leg to his back (b).

a

b

Chest and Arm Control

Grab your opponent's right arm with your right hand, then reach under his chest and grab your own wrist (a). Jump over to his right side and hip tilt him to that side (b). If he forces his hips back to the left to counter you, high gut wrench him back to his left side.

a

b

Index

N

O

P

Q

R

S

About the Authors

Mark Mysnyk was a two-time New York state high school champion, a member of four of the University of Iowa's NCAA championship teams, an alternate on the 1976 U.S. Olympic freestyle wrestling team, and a member of the 1977 World University team. His many years of wrestling and instructing wrestlers have provided him with the rich insights he shares in describing the techniques in this book. Dr. Mysnyk is an orthopedic surgeon in Iowa City and active as a volunteer wrestling coach with Cornell College in Mt. Vernon, Iowa. He is also the author of the highly successful book *Wrestling Fundamentals and Techniques: The Iowa Hawkeyes' Way*.

Brooks Simpson is a champion wrestler at the national level as a Big Ten champion and NCAA runner-up in 1990. He has taught wrestling techniques at Dan Gable's Training Camp and other wrestling clinics since 1986. He is the wrestling coach at Parkview High School in Springfield, Missouri.

Barry Davis has experienced success at every level of wrestling. He is a three-time NCAA champion; four-time All American; three-time Iowa state champion; and a Pan Am, World, and Olympic medalist. He also has several years' experience coaching wrestling as Dan Gable's assistant at the University of Iowa and as an assistant under Andy Rein at the University of Wisconsin. Barry is now the head wrestling coach at the University of Wisconsin.

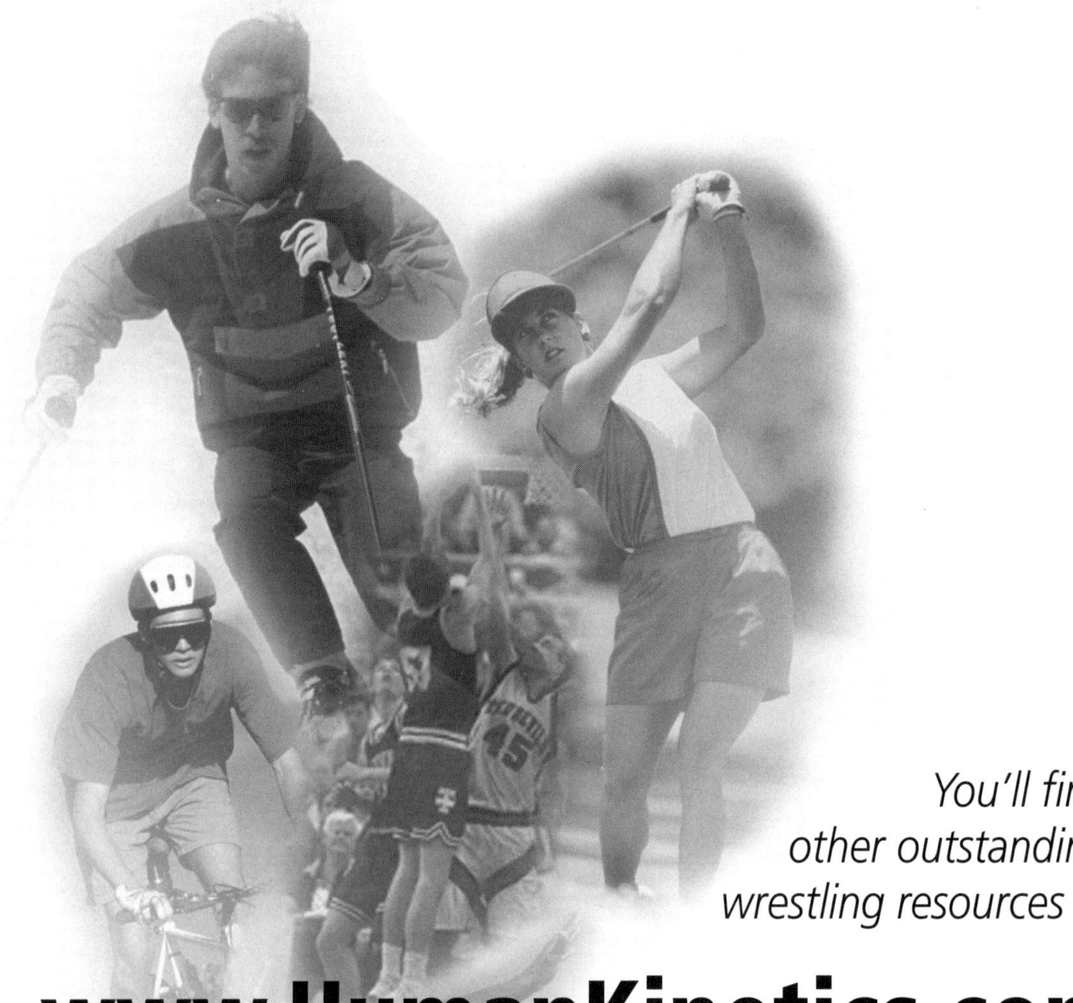